CONTENTS

HELLO AND WELCOME!

We're Amanda and Claire, the co-founders of If Lost Start Here®, a wellbeing company established to help you embrace the beautifully messy aspects of wellbeing and also the authors of this journal.

We're friends on a mission to help people find their way to a better place by providing accessible guidance for everyday life. Over the past ten years, we've explored what genuinely helps people navigate their lives, from books and podcasts to people and places. Driven by moments of feeling overwhelmed, anxious, or lost, we searched for and researched perspectives that help make life better and more fulfilling. We followed our curiosity everywhere.

What we discovered, not surprisingly, is that there's no single answer, quick-fix or method that we could wholeheartedly embrace. Instead, what was needed was a wellbeing approach unique to each person, one that can be shaped and amended as needed, something that moulds to an individual's life.

We also recognised that how we approach our own wellbeing needs to be attainable (people don't have time these days for long routines), kinder (there seems to be judgement in self-care), and playful (fun should be part of feeling better).

We've followed this approach ourselves, and worked through it with others, to help find balance, to reset, and to return to ourselves. Over the course of this journal, we'll help you create your own wellbeing practice to better navigate life in ways that feel meaningful to you.

This journal is designed to help you create your own wellbeing toolkit, a set of practices to anchor and support you when you feel lost, anxious or overwhelmed.

This journal will guide you in two ways:

- Inwardly: using journal prompts and self-coaching exercises, helping you explore your core values, beliefs and feelings.
- Outwardly: with challenges and life prompts, helping you find activities that ground you when you're uncertain and encourages you to explore when you're ready.

By using this journal you will create your own wellbeing practice and you'll have a clearer view of what matters, what works for you and how to integrate these into your life. So that you can move through your days in ways that align with who you are and what you need.

Life is what you make of it. This journal will reveal what that means for you.

We're excited to explore more of life with you. We hope you are too.

Love,

Claire & Amanda

Notes:

1. This journal is not a replacement for medical advice and is not suitable for anyone experiencing severe trauma or serious mental health challenges. This journal should not be used as a substitute for counselling, psychotherapy, psychoanalysis, mental health care, substance abuse treatment, or other professional advice by legal, medical or other qualified professionals.

2. If anything comes up over the course of this journal that you need additional support with, we encourage you to reach out to a coach, therapist or other mental health professional. A list of resources can be found on the website www.ifloststarthere.com.

3. Further reading and references can be found from page 193.

4. Many of the exercises can be repeated. Download further pages for printing from www.fromyoutome.com/freebies

7 WAYS THIS JOURNAL WILL HELP YOU

RECONNECT WITH YOURSELF: By using this journal you're creating boundaried time, stepping out of your everyday life for a moment and focusing on you in the 'now'. From the moment we wake up, it can often feel like the day slips away as we rush from one task to the next. The times when you open and use this journal, or undertake your challenges, are moments just for you.

FIND A PLACE TO START: Enabling you to craft a new beginning at any time. You do not need to wait until January or September to reset your days. This journal is your new blank page, your new beginning, to be opened at any moment of your choosing.

RE-ENGAGE WITH YOUR LIFE: Sometimes it can feel like life is on autopilot, that we're just doing the same things day in, day out. Following the stages in this journal will allow you to notice again, to discover possibilities, to try things that may be a stretch, to give things a go. Even if it feels a little uncomfortable to start with, it might also be fun to try something unexpected and create a new 'norm'.

CREATE YOUR DAYS: Often creativity is seen as being about making something. However, the principles of creativity can be applied to the very essence of our days, to shape and craft how we live our lives. We can scribble in the margins, we can shift perspective, we can cross out and add in, we can get playful in the story we are writing.

RESTORE SOMETHING THAT HAS BEEN LOST: Wherever you feel lost in life, this journal will help you find your way again. You'll be invited to become more open and curious to how you want to show up in your life, so that you can improve the foundations upon which your everyday wellbeing is built.

NOTICE WHERE NEEDS ATTENTION: Sometimes what we need is already somewhere in our lives, but it might live in a whisper. You'll be encouraged to find the aspects of your life that need some attention. We don't always need to change everything about ourselves or our lives to make it work better for us. So you'll get to evaluate your daily habits and see how they are (or aren't) serving you.

RESET AT ANY MOMENT: If you miss a day, an exercise, a challenge, that's OK. Just know that you can return to this journal anytime. We've found that it's extremely difficult to start, continue perfectly and then have a plan in place that lasts forever (even if that's our hope for ourselves). Life is about many necessary and frequent adjustments and resets that enable us to change direction ever so slightly and continue on our way.

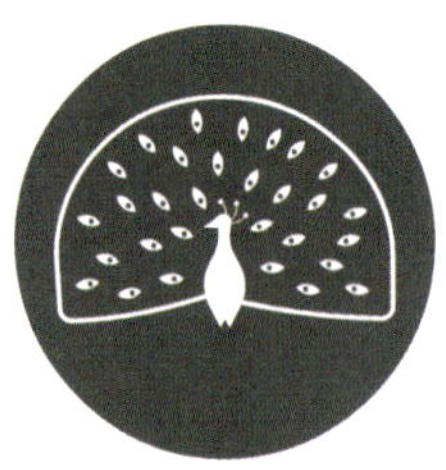

NATURE

CREATIVITY

CONNECTION

MIND & BODY

KINDNESS

PLAY & FUN

AWE & WONDER

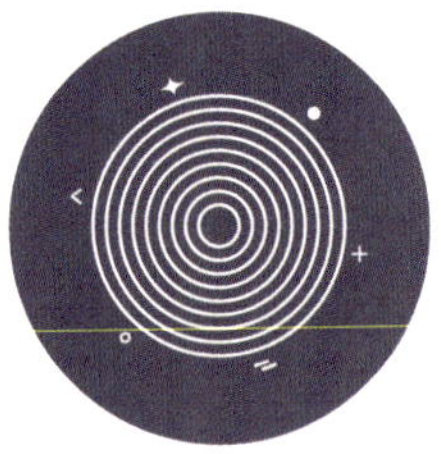

PURPOSE

SPIRITUALITY

UNTETHERING

GETTING STARTED

At If Lost Start Here® we believe that there are ten fundamental approaches to wellbeing which are outlined in the illustrations on page 6. We call these Pathways.

As you work through this journal you'll approach your life from multiple directions through these ten research-backed Pathways (for further reading, references by Pathway can be found on page 193). An easy way to use this journal is to commit to one Pathway a month so that you can work through the chapter and explore how this approach works for you. The science behind each Pathway is explained, along with the reasons why they might (or might not) matter to you, allowing you to move from awareness to action.

Before starting to explore the Pathways, the first section of this journal provides you with some guidance on journalling, a note on exploration and some ways to orientate yourself so that you get the most out of the process. You'll also find three activities, to focus on self-exploration allowing you to better understand what you are arriving with and what you are bringing. These are:

1. All About Me.
2. Commitment Capture.
3. Where I Am Right Now.

You'll then journey along each Pathway updating the handy tracker, on page 24, as you go. Each Pathway consists of inward activities, designed to help you explore your core values, beliefs and feelings including:

- The benefits of the Pathway.
- Determining where you are.
- A set of journal prompts.
- Self-coaching exercises.

And outward activities for engaging with life more, such as:

- Your mindset shift.
- A self-care challenge.
- A closing reflection.

There are prompts and exercises that take a few minutes, connecting activities that can be a day to a week long and other activities that you can keep returning to again and again. We just encourage you to do what you can with the time that you have.

Take what appeals to you - there is no failing in this journal, it's all just about exploration. Keep your mindset as curious as you can.

Depending on the commitment you make (and this may change over time) just remember to tweak and shift your focus according to your needs. Allow yourself to get curious about where you are, what you need and how you can build that into your everyday life so that it becomes a habit.

This journal is designed to help you identify your preferred way to create an everyday wellbeing practice of your own making.

Approach this journal like one of those 'Choose Your Own Adventure' books. Start working on the Pathways remembering that you can step forward if you need to, or come back later to exercises that you may struggle with.

Whilst we found that following the Pathways in the order they are set out in this journal is beneficial, you can move between the Pathways as you like, defining your own wellness journey based on your current areas of interest, needs and realities. When you have capacity, move forward with something, and when 'progress' feels a bit too much, focus on staying right where you are.

You can also choose the speed at which you move through this, although we do suggest you work through the Pathway over at least a 3-4 week period (we recommend a calendar month) so that exercises and challenges become habit forming. There are no specific dates, just your own time to see where this takes you and the opportunity to discover a foundational practice that will see you through all your days. Of course you can stay on a Pathway if you want to explore more, as you might just have found something magical that will serve you through your life.

Make this journal your own. We've provided the framework for thinking, doing and being, but you get to make your own. Complete the reflections, scribble notes, and work through the exercises. Make sure to add as much of yourself to the pages we've provided here.

Your path is unique . . .

A NOTE ON JOURNALLING

In this journal you'll find many writing prompts to build awareness and encourage self-reflection. Many people find that these prompts help them ask big questions and connect with their thoughts and feelings in ways they haven't before.

This is all about trusting yourself, becoming more aware of, and reconnecting with your inner voice. There's no right or wrong way, life can be busy, making it hard to take time for self-connection. Approach these prompts without self-judgement, aim to allocate yourself time. Journalling is about expressing how you think and feel, not crafting perfect sentences.

Sometimes, you might feel resistance to a question or struggle to answer it. That's OK, it's all part of the process and you can take as long as you need. Journalling helps process emotions, name your feelings and understand your needs. Research shows it can improve emotional wellbeing, reduce depression and even boost immune function. Writing can be a safe space to explore emotions such as grief, hope, courage or pride and build habits that strengthen our emotional resilience.

Take your time with the prompts, allowing whatever needs to unfold to do so. If writing feels difficult, try audio recordings or expressive drawing. Make it your own.

A NOTE ON EXPLORATION & DOING

Firstly there's the reflection part: building awareness and understanding where you are and want to be. Then there's the doing part, the moment you move into action. This journal encourages you to explore your everyday life, try new things, and re-engage with all life can offer. The activities help you embed learning, take chances and maybe get a little uncomfortable. Remember, no sailor learnt to sail on calm waters. By the end, you'll feel more connected with yourself, those you value, and the world around you.

For many people reflection can be undertaken anywhere. This often feels easier or safer than doing which often takes more effort. Or maybe you're a doer who spends little or no time reflecting, eager to fuel curiosity and fill your moments. If this is the case, then reflecting may involve a change of pace and we encourage you not to rush this stage.

Neither is right nor wrong: notice where you are and how to balance if needed; wander down a new path. Leaving your comfort zone is hard, but beauty and wonder await when you explore. As you step along the Pathways, ask yourself: "How can I best orientate myself so I get the most out of this process?"

SOME WAYS TO . . .

CURIOSITY

We invite you to explore, try, and be open to what's possible in each Pathway. As you move through, ask yourself: What resonates with me? What do I need? What do I not need?

Seeking offers something valuable. Often, we're doing everything for everyone, and taking this time helps us connect with what we truly need now.

Giving ourselves a moment to explore, feed our curiosity and listen to what we think and feel can offer much of what we're longing for.

For this journal to feel right, it needs to feel like exploring as much as learning. Stay curious, not judgemental and be kind to yourself as you navigate what belongs to you, others or something systemic.

Our mantra: "I will follow my curiosity wherever it takes me."

CREATIVITY

View this journal as your invitation, your space to play. Get creative with how you approach your wellbeing. Bring your brightest pens. An open mind. See your life as a blank page. Bring some things that you might never have considered, allow yourself to experiment (to even fail), don't look for the perfect answer.

When we bring a spirit of creativity, when we allow ourselves to play, we give ourselves not just space for trying, but also forgiveness when we get something wrong.

Also, have you found that all this talk of better wellbeing can get a little bit boring: it's all terribly serious, sometimes even self-righteous.

We're not about bringing more judgement to either you or anyone else. We can bring the fun back to wellness.

Our mantra: "It's OK to play and have fun."

ORIENTATE YOURSELF

COMPASSION

We encourage you to approach this journal with a tone of compassion and acceptance. What you eat and how many burpees you can do does not define your self-worth. Not having a morning routine is absolutely fine. Finding meditation frustrating does not mean you've failed.

We need to realise that the person drinking green juice and meditating is not a better person than the one who isn't. This journal doesn't aim to change everything about who you are.

And let's also check in with what it is you are ready to accept about yourself?

What's something you don't want to change about yourself and your life?

Our mantra: "I will throw away any self-judgement."

COMMUNITY

We believe that we can and need to shift from self-help to a form of collective care. Often, we share similar concerns and needs, but we often do this alone. This is where we come together, because connection is a huge part of what we're looking to (re-)discover.

We've built a community on socials where you'll be able to chat with us about what comes up for you as you complete this journal, to share your learnings and insights, what inspires you, how you found a challenge, a question that changed everything . . .

We're open to any feedback and suggestions that can support our mission to help as many people as possible with their everyday wellbeing.

In the spirit of community, buy a second journal to gift and do this with a friend. We do life better, together.

Our mantra: "I will join the community, supporting myself & others."

ALL ABOUT ME
What's My Starting Point?

When planning any journey it's good to know where you are starting from. So let's start with where you are now. Where's your beginning? Why are you here? What are you bringing with you and what do you want to leave behind?

What brings you here? What would you like a wellbeing practice to do for you?

What are you hoping to move towards?

What's significant about that in your life at the moment?

What values do you hold around wellbeing?

Values are those things you find most important like safety, curiosity & belonging.

What beliefs do you hold about wellbeing and you?

Beliefs are the things you hold to be true about yourself e.g. I deserve this.

What feelings do you currently have about wellbeing?

Feelings could be excitement or fear, shame or optimism.

A Note On Mindset Shifting: In her research, psychologist Carol S. Dweck has found that our mindsets matter in how we approach the world. Adopting 'a growth mindset' where we believe that we have the capacity to learn and develop ourselves rather than a 'fixed mindset' where we believe that our traits are static and we are who we are, can help better support us as we nurture ourselves, reach our goals, learn and grow.

My Wellbeing Goals

Capture anything that you'd like to work towards. You can refine these later as you learn & experience more.

I believe a wellbeing practice can . . .

My four goals for my wellbeing practice are . . .

Examples could be: to restore my energy, to connect more, to feel healthier and happier, etc.

2
COMMITMENT CAPTURE
What's My Dedication Level?

Well done, you've started to shape your goals. Our invitation is to spend a moment figuring out what level of commitment you'll be bringing (there's no right amount, no one level that is correct - we don't know your life as you do).

Ask yourself the following questions:

* Am I just going to read the pages so I can reframe my position on something?
* Am I going to try at least one new thing, integrate one new idea each month?
* Am I going to journal each day?
* Something else?

Here's a Commitment Capture: you can reassess this as you work through this journal and get clearer on the Pathways. Start to note the different ways in which moving through this journal can feel good to you.

What level of commitment am I prepared to bring?
(Bring some generosity to this question as you answer this.)

How do I want to go about it?
What are my commitment strategies going to be?

What might get in the way? What will I do when that happens?
(Bring some self-compassion as you answer this one.)

How will I come back to this when life gets in the way (it will and that's totally OK).

How can I get the most out of this so it feels good, as well as impactful?

WHERE I AM RIGHT NOW

At If Lost Start Here® we believe that there are ten fundamental approaches to wellbeing. All or some of these will become the foundations for your own everyday practice.

UNTETHERING

NATURE

CREATIVITY

SPIRITUALITY

In this exercise you'll identify which of the ten Pathways to wellbeing matter most to you at this stage in the process.

Then you'll explore which ones you want to bring into your life and what you need right now to help remake (or slightly tweak) your world.

CONNECTION

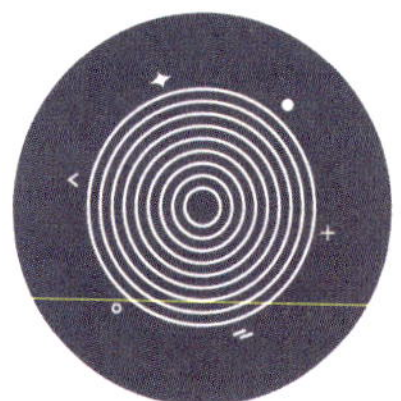

PURPOSE

MIND & BODY

AWE & WONDER

PLAY & FUN

KINDNESS

1
DEFINING MY WAY

We all bring with us assumptions, biases and expectations to these Pathways, please note your initial reactions to each.

NATURE

What is nature for you?

CREATIVITY

What does creativity mean to you?

CONNECTION

What does connection bring up?

MIND & BODY

What does mind & body suggest to you?

KINDNESS

What comes to mind with kindness?

PLAY & FUN

Where does your mind go with an idea of play?

AWE

What do you associate with awe & wonder?

PURPOSE

What does purpose mean to you?

SPIRITUALITY

What does the idea of spirituality conjure?

UNTETHERING

What are your thoughts on tech & you?

2
ORIENTATION

This journal will explain each Pathway in detail later. For now, simply look at each one and decide how present it feels in your life at this moment. Then add a mark in each section to show your score. You'll get the opportunity to do this again; you're just recording where you are right now. Further charts are available to download from www.fromyoutome.com/freebies.

The outer dot is the highest score (10) and the inner dot is the lowest score (1). For example, if your life is full of positive creativity, you'd maybe score creativity a 10. If your life is tethered to tech, you'd maybe score Untethering a 1 or 2. Complete the chart using a pen to join up your marks to create a web.

3
QUICK CHECK-IN

What stood out
for me the most?

Where am I
out of balance?

What do I care
about already that
I'd like to keep in my
wellbeing practice?

Now look at your
wellbeing goals from
page 16. Has anything
shifted?

What's Next? Did we mention how happy we are that you are here? We're excited you're taking this time for yourself to design your wellbeing practice for everyday life so that you (and probably those around you too) can have more good days. Before you begin exploring the Pathways you can update the tracker on the next page and come back to it each time you complete one as a record of how well you are doing. The first Pathway is one of our favourites as we've found it to be the remedy for tired souls.

4
KEEPING TRACK

In this section you will be able to keep track of how you are doing and you will be able to date and score when you have completed a specific Pathway.

DATE COMPLETED   SCORE

ALL ABOUT ME

NATURE

CREATIVITY

CONNECTION

MIND & BODY

KINDNESS

Score each Pathway. 10 - I loved it! to 1 - I really struggled, and everywhere in between. This helps identity where you may need to do more work and where you can thrive.

PLAY & FUN

AWE & WONDER

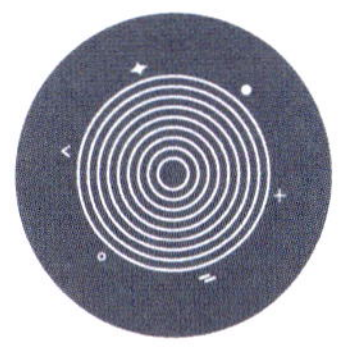

PURPOSE

SPIRITUALITY

UNTETHERING

DEFINING A WAY
FORWARD

I DID IT!

"The beauty of the natural world, especially the beauty of flowers, can sometimes reawaken a love of life."

– Sue Stuart-Smith –

BRINGING IN NATURE

NATURE

Welcome to your first Pathway! Here, you'll explore the connection between wellbeing and nature.

You'll learn that a relationship with nature is fundamental to wellbeing and its absence can be just as impactful.

Many of us have felt, and struggled with, a growing distance from the natural world. As we've become busier in our lives, we've forgotten, or lost (or misplaced, like our keys) what is going on outside and all around us.

We've become absorbed in our minds, in our urban/suburban spaces, in days and nights that have nothing to do with seasons or sunlight. We're no longer taking time to notice the world around us often enough.

We've stopped integrating green and blue spaces, wild settings where we once thrived, into our lives. Our gazes have shifted from upwards to downwards, from skies to phones, from moments in nature to daily to-dos.

People rarely appreciate how vital daily walks and time outdoors are, noticing seasonal wild flowers, bird songs, and the changing colours of the seasons. Simple activities such as going for a 30-minute walk, doing a bit of gardening, watching the birds or even cold water swimming are ways to rewild our lives, even just a little.

In this Pathway you'll revive or cultivate your relationship with nature. No need for a National Park or special gear, this is about micro-gestures: stepping outside; walking instead of driving; noticing the sky or re-orienting your gaze to greenery.

Nature isn't the same thing for everyone. For some, green fields or trails can feel intimidating or unreachable. If that's you, don't worry. Nature can mean planting indoor gardens rather than multi-day hikes. The first step is finding what feels good to you.

Whatever your starting point you are invited to be more nature-curious, to explore how it supports emotional wellbeing and improved mental health.

Let's bring intention to time in nature and see where it leads . . .

BENEFITS OF NATURE

In recent studies, it has been identified that people vastly undervalue the role nature plays in their mental wellbeing. But research suggests time and again, that being in nature offers more than just a burst of fresh air and a pretty view: it may actually hold the key to restoring our long-lost sense of equilibrium.

We now know that the human brain and body react to nature in ways that enhance our sense of connection, reduce pain, and allow us to experience a deep sense of calm.

Additionally, time in nature has been shown to lower blood pressure, increase immunity, boost creativity, reduce anxiety and depression, improve concentration and work satisfaction, and even reduce crime rates. Even looking at pictures of nature can help us feel better.

DETERMINING WHERE YOU ARE

Maybe you associate nature with running from cows and stepping over bugs, or of being by a blissful stream, feet dangling, clouds meandering overhead? Perhaps the mud under your boots feels better than the asphalt beneath your shoes ever could.

You may be more comfortable in a concrete jungle with a thousand people around or floundering down country lanes and wondering what's around the bend in the path.

Wherever you are, we've found that we are always profoundly in relationship with nature: scared of it, longing for it, curious about it, avoiding it, but needing it in some form all the same.

How did you rate yourself on the wheel on page 22 and now think about where you want to be? Take this into account as you move through the Pathway. Keep checking back if you need to.

Note where you are on the map below if this is helpful.

WHAT IS NATURE FOR YOU?

Though we want to get you outside as soon as possible, spend a moment completing these journal prompts.

What comes to mind when you think about nature?

What are some of your feelings about it?

What associations does it have for you?

What's getting in the way of being in nature for you?

How can you help yourself have a closer relationship with nature?

Note one thing, just one, that excites you about nature.

What compels you to shift something in this area?

Who might you share this with?

What's the relationship you want to have with nature?

NOTICE THE NATURAL WORLD

Now it's time to go outside, take a snack if you like, and try the practice below. Make notes as you go. Do it once or do it daily to create a pattern.

5 things you can see

4 things you can hear

3 things you can feel

2 things you can smell

1 thing you can taste e.g. your snack. What did you choose?

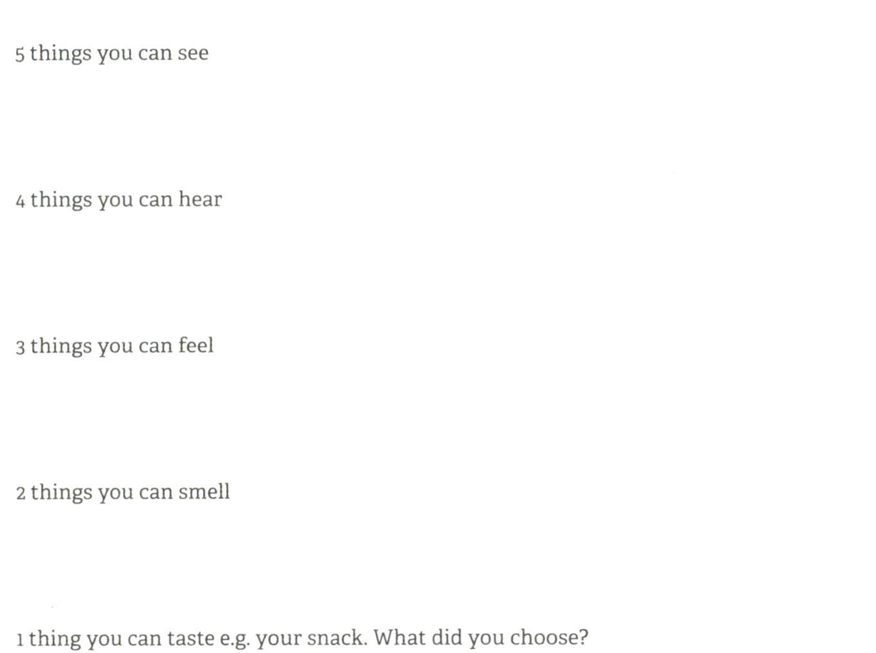

NOTICE THE SEASONS

What season is it?

As you step outside, or look out the window, what do you notice about the season you are in?

What can you look forward to about the next season? What will it bring that's different?

YOUR MINDSET SHIFT

GET OUTSIDE EACH DAY FOR 30 MINUTES

If you need to, start with 10 minutes a day and build up to at least 30. The most important part is to really take in what you can experience. Look up, around, and down. Notice nature, whether it's a weed between a pavement crack (what resilience they show!) or distant hills, birdsong or tree-lined roads. Wherever you are, aim to find some beauty in the glimpses of nature that you discover.

How would you describe your current mindset about this Pathway?

What do you currently believe about this?

What do you need to change to shift this belief?

What learning is opening up for you?

What steps could you take, or experiences could you try to shift your mindset?

YOUR CHALLENGE

Explore ways to reconnect with nature - start small and see what inspires you!

Use these prompts to help you view nature as accessible and within reach, not as something distant. Choose prompts to incorporate into everyday life, remembering just two hours a week can unlock nature's benefits.

You can even create your own ideas for bringing nature into daily life. Small, consistent steps build a healthier, more connected you.

- [ ] Find a lovely spot to sit in a local park or green area.
- [ ] Seek out a safe wild-swimming spot. Share it with a friend.
- [ ] Try a new hike or walk.
- [ ] Learn the name of the trees you often see.
- [ ] Buy and plant bulbs from a local garden centre.
- [ ] Take out your headphones and listen to the birds.
- [ ] Ditch the car and go on a walk from home.
- [ ] Identify a space you regularly overlook. Can you help bring it to life?
- [ ] See beauty in the weeds/reframe the wild/notice nature around you.
- [ ] Help look after the garden of someone struggling to do so.
- [ ] Join a community allotment.
- [ ] Go camping in your home town (even if it's just your garden).
- [ ] Look up upcoming green volunteering days and attend one.
- [ ] Discover a place you can only walk to.
- [ ] Take your workout outdoors.
- [ ] Join (or start) a walking or rambling club.
- [ ] Seek out a wild sauna.
- [ ] Go beachcombing.
- [ ] Take a walk (or dance) in the rain.
- [ ] Invite a friend to share outside activity with you.

YOUR NATURE PATHWAY

As you come to the end of this Pathway, we hope you take away the possibility that there are ways that nature can easily fit into your everyday life in ways that benefit your emotional and mental wellbeing. That there's a space for the natural world, whether that's just the attention you pay to it when you do go outside, or how you proactively seek it out when you're able.

Write down your learnings from exploring this Pathway ...

How will you fit nature into your wellbeing practice for everyday life?

What's something you've really enjoyed or are excited to try/do?

YOUR WELLBEING PRACTICE BUILDER

As you move through this journal, allow your wellbeing practice to slowly build so that it is embedded in your daily life and encompasses all that you need in order to thrive. The trick is that it is all forever shifting, so there really is no 'arrival', just a lifetime of resetting your course. These Pathways are always there to lead you back to yourself, and to what matters most to you. We'll meet you in the next Pathway crafted entirely for you (hint: there's a clue there).

Don't forget to update your Pathway tracker on page 24.

GET OUTSIDE

"When you're not making stuff,
there's this part of you that aches,
but you don't know why it aches."

– Lisa Congdon -

EXPLORING CREATIVITY

CREATIVITY

Hooray! You've made it to the next Pathway!

It may have taken you a couple of weeks or a couple of months (no judgement here!) to embed the first Pathway into your life. It really doesn't matter how long you take. We're just glad you're exploring what matters and developing your unique wellbeing practice that feels right for you.

In this second Pathway, you'll focus on bringing more creativity into your everyday life. Creativity can take multiple forms, from making paintings to writing songs or working on your memoir. It could be that improvisation class you are curious to try or that pottery workshop you've yet to attend.

Your mind will probably go somewhere, to a craft you're most interested to explore. But it might also lead you to recall all those things you've come to believe about your creativity. Creativity often gets tied to being 'good' at something or having 'talent'. This can invite judgement not only of ourselves ('my drawing isn't good enough') but also of a perceived assessment by others ('they dislike my work').

This is called 'the inner critic', which may have been cultivated by experience: the art teacher who said, 'never draw again', or the family member dismissing art as indulgent. Let's silence those voices by letting them fall away, allowing your innate creativity to fill the space instead. This may feel uncomfortable, but think of it as practising a new way of being with yourself, using creativity as a safe space.

Here, creativity is all about the process and how it makes you feel. It's about accessing its positive benefits for emotional and mental wellbeing.
Set aside assumptions about expertise or ability and see how making something, whether movements or marks, songs or paintings can bring meaning to our lives.

Creativity isn't just for professionals, you don't have to be the next Michelangelo or Monet. It's also OK if all you want to do is appreciate other peoples work. You may find in this Pathway that creativity isn't just about what you love to make but also about how you like to engage with the work of others, the vast cultural possibilities offered by museums and galleries, live music venues and cinemas, opera houses and theatres that offer their own wellbeing benefits too.

Expand both your own creative practice and the places you seek to inspire you. Both have the capacity to help us feel better in our everyday life.

This Pathway explores how creativity might help you feel better and more connected to yourself. Whether creativity becomes a cornerstone of your wellbeing or something you set aside, both are good. So grab your brightest pens and, most of all, an open mind and explore.

There's no such thing as a mistake . . . it's all creative!

BENEFITS OF CREATIVITY

There has been a burst of interest in creativity and all the positive impacts that it can have on our everyday life and emotional wellbeing.

Recent research suggests incorporating creativity into our wellbeing practice can make us happier and healthier. Studies have shown that creativity can help alleviate depression, anxiety and stress, and engaging with the arts has been related to a greater sense of wellbeing.

Knitting, for instance, has been shown to positively impact mood, while therapeutic writing has been shown to help people de-stress, improve low self-esteem and alleviate loss and grief. Even museums are exploring their potential as therapeutic spaces.

DETERMINING WHERE YOU ARE

Let's figure out where you are in relation to creativity. For some this may be daunting, for others they will already be rushing for their brushes.

At school your art teacher may have crushed beloved dreams. Making art of any kind can feel indulgent and not at all grown-up or possibly even terrifying! Is there a barrier between you and creativity? This could take the shape of self-doubt, comparison to others, not giving yourself permission to relax into it, or a perfectionism that results in it being hard to even try. Some of this might be driven by Imposter Syndrome, the belief that you will be found out for not being 'good enough'.

This is me ☐

Or, when you're in a creative space you are often in a state of flow, where time runs away from you. You don't even notice that it's been two hours and you've been writing or painting or knitting, but it feels like it's been five minutes. Life makes sense again.

This is me ☐

How did you rate yourself on the wheel on page 22 and now think about where you want to be? Take this into account as you move through the Pathway. Keep checking back if you need to.

Note where you are on the map below if this is helpful.

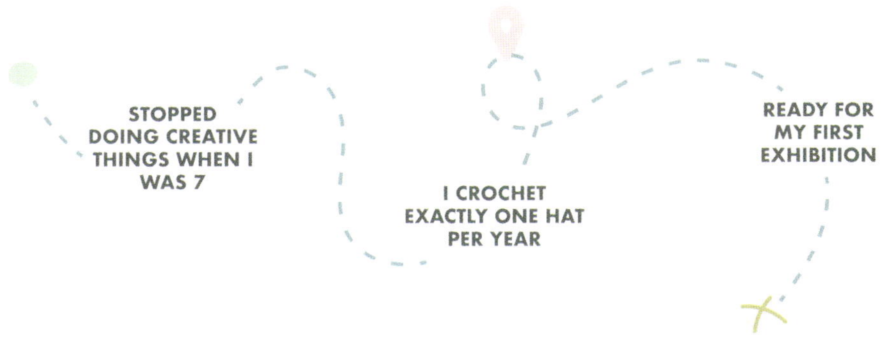

WHAT IS CREATIVITY FOR YOU?

As this Pathway is all about understanding what creativity looks like for you, you're invited to treat these journal prompts a little differently. You can still write your responses. However, you can also draw, paint or even doodle musical notes to capture where you are in relation to these questions. Whatever medium appeals to you, no one will see it, it's entirely for you what you create. What images/words/melodies/movements come to mind when you're invited to think about the role creativity plays in your life?

What does creativity mean to you?

In what ways do you consider yourself to be a creative person?

How does creativity show up in your life right now? How would you like it to show up?

What fuels your creativity? What drains it?

How can you let your creativity lead the way? Where would it take you?

Are you noticing any resistance to exploring your own creativity?

How might creativity be connected to your mental health or emotional wellbeing?

YOUR SPACE TO GET CREATIVE

Imagine creativity itself. What does that look like to you? And how would you depict where you are in relation to it - are you a tiny person squeezed into the corner of a page or the conductor up front and centre, making magic happen?

Does creativity conjure up images of something devouring you, or do you picture all sparks and rocket ships and flying with it to the moon? Maybe you just see a blank page or a blinking cursor or a whole bookshelf of your bestsellers.

Here's an empty space. What will you do with it? Write a micro story, doodle a dream, make a noughts-and-crosses board, sketch out a fashion design.

Explore your natural way to engage your creativity: words and images or something that takes you beyond these pages to other creative mediums . . .

YOUR MINDSET SHIFT

EMBRACE YOUR CREATIVITY

Being 'creative' can come with so much baggage, but what if we treated creativity itself as a blank page. What would that make space for? Re-orientate your practice away from what you make to why you make and how it makes you feel - see if that shifts anything in you. Approach your creativity with a sense of play and curiosity.

How would you describe your current mindset about this Pathway?

What do you currently believe about this?

What do you need to change to shift this belief?

What learning is opening up for you?

What steps could you take, or experiences could you try to shift your mindset?

YOUR CHALLENGE

Now that you've explored how creativity impacts your wellbeing, let's dive into practical ways to weave it into daily life. This isn't about perfection or pressure, it's about playing, experimenting, and finding what inspires you. Creativity doesn't need to look a certain way; it's for you and you alone. How can you embrace creativity as a practice for wellbeing?

Explore the ideas below or create your own prompts to get started!

- [ ] Discover a new artwork in a local gallery.
- [ ] Make something in a craft workshop.
- [ ] Book a ticket to a local theatre production.
- [ ] Listen to an author talk at a community bookshop.
- [ ] Learn the stories of public artworks in your community.
- [ ] Join local community initiatives to make your world more beautiful.
- [ ] Support a library.
- [ ] Take a sketchbook (or even a camera) with you on a local walk.
- [ ] Allow yourself to get bored. See if that sparks anything.
- [ ] Sing. In the shower. With friends. On your commute. Or join a choir.
- [ ] Make something new with the things lying around your house.
- [ ] Combine Pathways and make something with, in or for Nature.
- [ ] Host a crafting night with your friends.
- [ ] Support an indie/artisan's makers' market.
- [ ] Write a poem, short story, screenplay, essay (no one has to read it).
- [ ] Just doodle, pen on paper, no creative goal in mind.
- [ ] Listen to a new genre of music.
- [ ] Try a creative practice you've never explored e.g. paint, sculpt, collage.
- [ ] Make something analogue from beloved digital photos.
- [ ] If in doubt, dance. Kitchen micro discos allowed.

YOUR CREATIVITY PATHWAY

It's now time to create your guide to life. Capture any thoughts or insights from this Pathway and explore how making and wellbeing might intertwine in your daily life. Creativity could become your anchor, or maybe it's not for you - and that's OK too.

How might creativity fit within your wellbeing practice for everyday life?

What's something you're excited to try/implement/do?

What's something you're ready to leave behind?

INTEGRATING

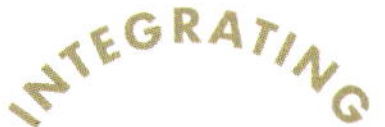

YOUR WELLBEING PRACTICE BUILDER

In this Pathway you're mostly in relationship with yourself. In the next we're going to see what happens when you are in the company of others. We're leaving the studio (metaphorical or otherwise) for someone . . . who that is, you get to decide.

See you in the next Pathway. Until then we'll be getting messy with all kinds of materials as we seek out enlightenment . . .

Don't forget to update your Pathway tracker on page 24.

GET OUTSIDE

EMBRACE YOUR CREATIVITY

INVEST IN YOUR RELATIONSHIPS

MOVE FOR YOUR MIND

ORIENT YOUR LIFE TO KIND

LEAN INTO FUN

RE-ENCHANT YOUR EVERYDAY LIFE

LIVE WITH YOUR WHY

EXPLORE WITH GRACE

RE-EVALUATE YOUR LIFE WITH TECH

“It is the quality of your relationships which ultimately determine the quality of your life.”

– Esther Perel –

FINDING CONNECTION

CONNECTION

You've arrived at the Connection Pathway. Things will be shifting a little as we connect with other people in your life by focusing on the importance of interpersonal relationships for your everyday wellbeing.

We'll identify where you can catch yourself if you're maybe feeling lonely. We'll increase your awareness of when you tip into too much isolation and when you need to reach out or make more of an effort with the people around you. Lastly we'll be finding ways to be grateful for those you already spend your days with, honouring the most important relationships in your life.

We are hard-wired to be around people. This Pathway is about finding ways for connection to be an active and sustainable practice that speaks to your needs, temperament and capacity, so that you can nurture your relationships the same way you would other aspects of your life. Think of it as social fitness.

Don't worry though, we're not advocating for a one-size-fits-all way of being in the world, with an open-door policy on who is let in and how often. For people with introversion tendencies, being constantly around others can take its toll. We don't want to invite in the discomfort that can come from trying to be something you're not and depleting your social battery.

For people with extroversion tendencies, you get your energy from being around others. Remember one of the questions you're answering as part of this journal is to identify where you feel good. That might just be here, in this Pathway; and it's something to cultivate and sustain in a healthy way throughout your life.

Being diverse in how we respond to the world socially is OK, we just need to ascertain the levels at which we function best. The quality of our connections matter. You might feel lonely in a room full of people or with your partner. You may feel happy in your own company. However, everyone needs some sense of social interaction, so you may need to work out if you have a tendency for avoidance. Or you might love being around people but find yourself in a kind of relational burn-out, always switched on.

We might think of human connection as only about romantic and platonic love, but it can also be about reminding ourselves that the small interactions with those around us, like with the barista at the local café or your co-workers, are more impactful than they may seem. Even talking to strangers has been found to help us feel better.

Connection is also about how we show up in our communities, whether that's where we live or work, in spaces of shared interests including sports or music, hobbies like crafts or gaming, or values and beliefs, such as faith-based groups. Belonging to a wider group can offer the support that we all need through the good times and the bad. So we'll be finding ways for you to re-engage with where you live and contribute to the places you call home, whatever that looks like for you.

So whether you are still hanging out or holding back, going out or scrolling, taking some social risks or ordering everything you can through an app, our question is this: How do you really feel about your relationships, and how connection (and community) currently show up in your everyday life?

BENEFITS OF CONNECTION

As humans, we are social creatures, and our need for connection is deeply ingrained. Strong social connection has many benefits for our wellbeing. Like reducing anxiety and depression, strengthening our immune system and helping us recover from disease faster. Healthy human connection has even been shown to lengthen our lives.

The evidence that's often quoted around the power of human connection is from the Harvard Study of Adult Development. Since 1938, this study has tracked the wellbeing of its participants and determined that the most important contributor to health and happiness levels is the quality of our relationships. Simply put, living in the midst of warm relationships is protective of both mind and body.

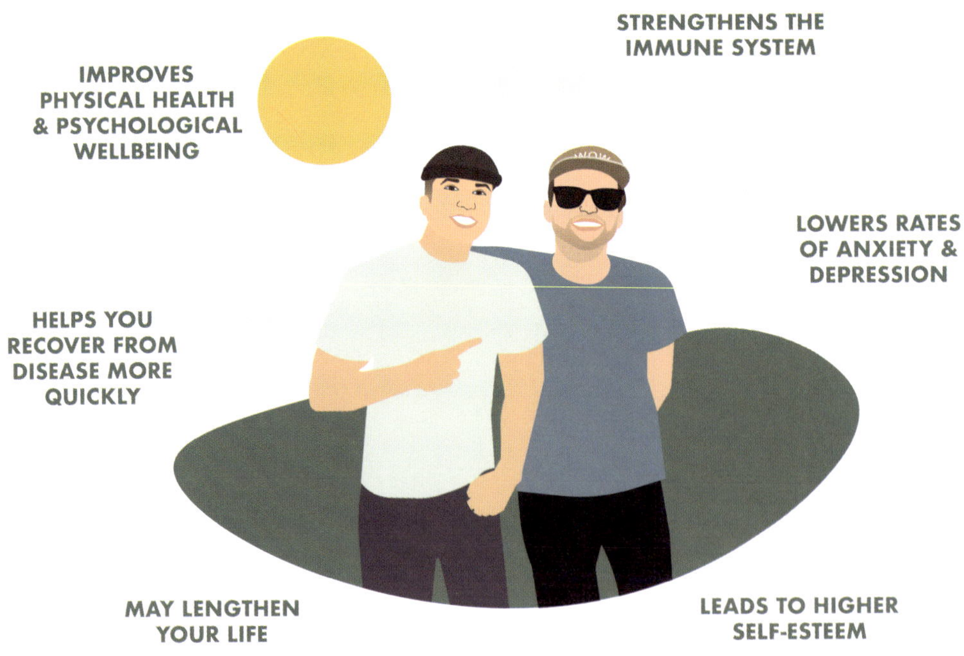

DETERMINING WHERE YOU ARE

The former US Surgeon General Dr. Vivek Murthy has identified a current epidemic of loneliness which threatens public health as much as obesity and tobacco. He suggested that a lack of social interaction is bad for our health and as damaging as smoking 15 cigarettes a day. Tending to our friendships has been found to be just as important to our mental health as a good night's sleep and eating well.

For some, solitude is a happy place, for others, they need to be in the centre of a buzzing room yelling to be heard and stepping on toes. Some seek out a handful of meaningful relationships, while others collect friendships like shoes, chosen according to occasion and mood. Some have too many people in their lives, many not enough.

The number of people we need is subjective. Some may feel like they don't have enough social connections in their lives (indicating social loneliness), others might feel lonely in their existing relationships (more emotional loneliness). Some people might be content with a handful of close friends who they see occasionally, others need a wider social network who they socialise with often. We all function a little differently, but for all of us social connection is vital to physical and mental health. No matter how we feel about people, we still need them. In this Pathway, you'll be measuring your social temperature. Asking yourself - where, and with whom, am I happiest?

How did you rate yourself on the wheel on page 22 and now think about where you want to be? Take this into account as you move through the Pathway. Keep checking back if you need to.

Note where you are on the map below if this is helpful.

WHAT IS CONNECTION FOR YOU?

There is absolutely no judgement to how you answer today's journal prompts. There can be a stigma around loneliness as well as some baggage around 'popularity'. There can be some sense that everyone else is having so much fun together at their meet-ups and weekends away. Put all that aside, because this is about you (and there's no-one peering over your shoulder). Bring compassion rather than comparison to this space. If you are happy with how you connect with others, use these journal prompts to explore how to savour these relationships and enjoy all that they bring you.

How do you feel about connecting with people?

How do you find yourself moving towards people?
And when do you find yourself moving away from them?

How do you show the people in your life that you care about them?

What's the definition of a good friend to you?

How would you like to nurture your relationships with a good friend this month?

How do you see yourself as part of your community where you live?

How would you like to connect more with your community?

What can you contribute to your community?

CONNECTION

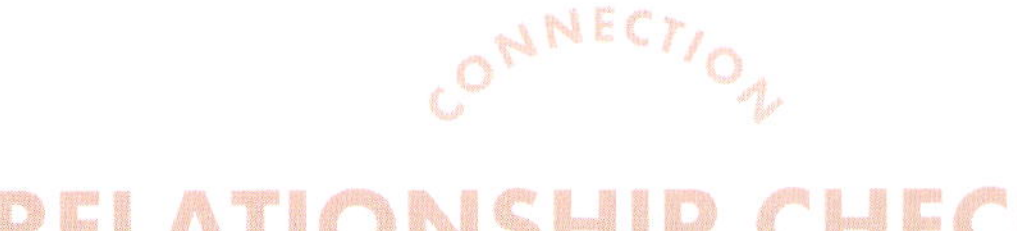

RELATIONSHIP CHECK-IN

This adaptation of 'The Circle Of Friends' exercise involves adding the names of people to each of the circles depending on where they currently sit within your life. Explore any learnings from this on the next few pages and take them into account how you approach this Pathway.

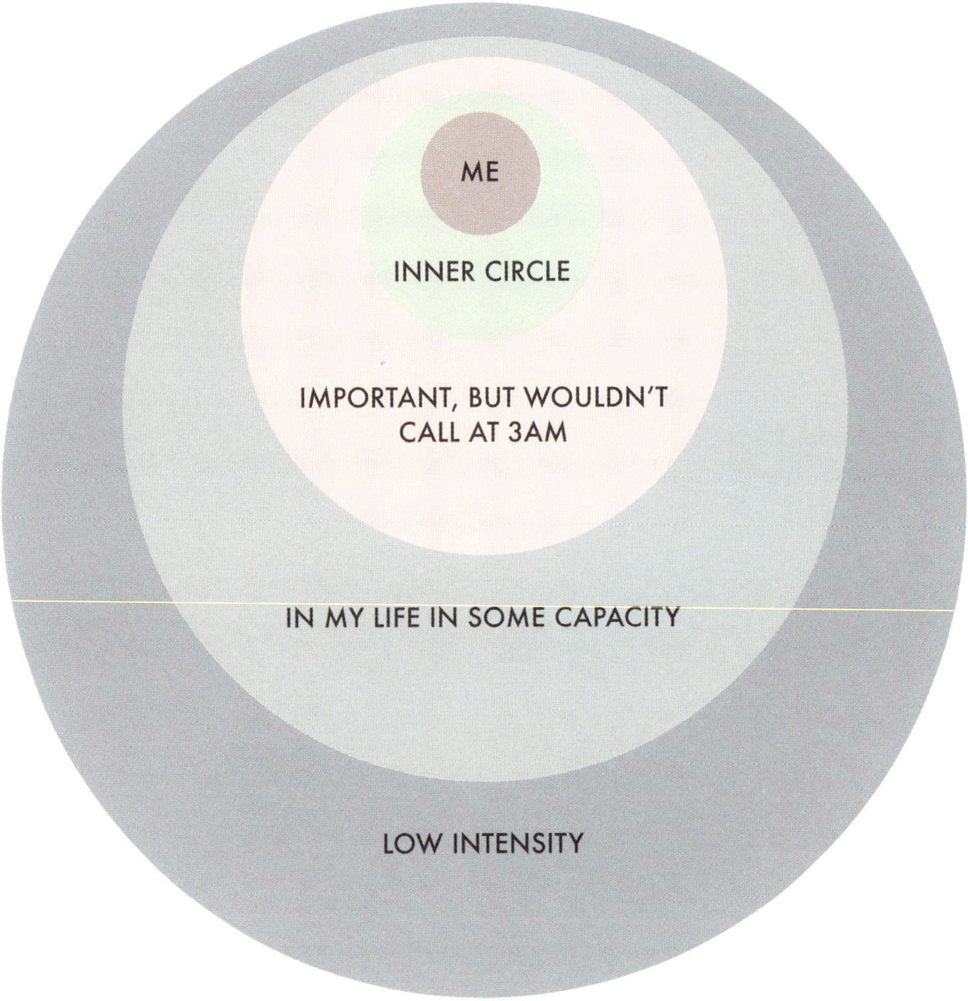

INNER CIRCLE: Your shoulders to cry on, the romantic partner, close friend or family member who you can rely on for support and you'd tell almost anything to.

IMPORTANT BUT WOULDN'T CALL AT 3 IN THE MORNING: These are your good friends, the trusted colleague and family members who you enjoy spending time with.

IN MY LIFE IN SOME CAPACITY: Everyone else who you come into contact with or you may call friends, but you wouldn't share your vulnerabilities or secrets.

LOW INTENSITY: These are your most casual friends and acquaintances who you interact with, your professional contacts, community members and neighbours.

What did you find? Is the inner circle more empty than you'd like?
Or do you have many intimate relationships, but fewer peripheral social connections?
When you look at this, how do you feel about where people sit?

How is this different to how you imagined it?

Where are there gaps you'd like to fill? Where can you bring in more of a boundary?

How would you like to invite in more or less connection?

Who is in your support network? How would you like to develop that network?

Complete these sentences:

I'd like to spend more time with . . .

I'd like to find people who I have a shared interest around . . .

YOUR MINDSET SHIFT

INVEST IN YOUR RELATIONSHIPS

People often come last. We have so much to do that the phone call can wait, the dinner can be rescheduled, that conversation can happen tomorrow. We binge watch Netflix because it feels easier than talking, we avoid eye contact on our commute, we order our coffee on an app for convenience. But what if we re-peopled our world? In this mindset shift, you'll explore how to nurture the people you want and need in your life. We need to invest time and energy on all the different social groups/muscle groups, whether that's family, friends, neighbours, partners, co-workers or just the person who hands you your coffee.

How would you describe your current mindset about this Pathway?

What do you currently believe about this?

What do you need to change to shift this belief?

What learning is opening up for you?

What steps could you take, or experiences could you try, to shift your mindset?

YOUR CHALLENGE

Explore ways to invite people into your life or set boundaries when needed. You don't have to do all the prompts, just follow what inspires you. Connection can take many forms from small talk, meaningful relationships, or shared activities that create bonds. Add connecting with people to your to-do list and see what magic unfolds.

- ☐ Hang out with your friends (the offline ones).
- ☐ Make a phone call 80s-style.
- ☐ Invite friends for brunch & bring curiosity questions in advance.
- ☐ Prioritise a friendship this week.
- ☐ Shop locally, get to know the people behind independent businesses.
- ☐ Join a local sports team or even pick one to support.
- ☐ Handwrite a letter and send it to someone you care about.
- ☐ Plan a cinema date with friends, neighbours and/or people at work.
- ☐ Join or host a community picnic, a pot-luck gathering or BBQ.
- ☐ Talk to someone who you suspect might be feeling lonely.
- ☐ Volunteer for a befriending service.
- ☐ Try a day at a co-working space.
- ☐ Invite a neighbour to dinner.
- ☐ Send a card if you've been meaning to message a friend.
- ☐ Join a friend on a walk, shopping for groceries, or running an errand.
- ☐ Identify a place where you feel you belong.
- ☐ Join or start a book, podcast, or film club.
- ☐ Try one new thing pinned to a community notice board.
- ☐ Take a friend to a new event/place you've been wanting to try.
- ☐ Share some great local places with friends. Ask them to share theirs.

YOUR CONNECTION PATHWAY

We are constantly in relationship with other people, but ironically this is one area we often neglect as life presses in and we often take those close to us for granted.

Connection can be difficult, as we all hold some assumptions about who we need to be, and who others need to be, before we can show up in relationships or our communities. So, let's check some of that emotional baggage and ask yourself this:

What could a life of positive human connection look like for you? From this Pathway what are you learning about how you feel and what you need? Could you shift just a little where connection falls on your agenda for everyday life and make it part of your wellbeing practice?

Connection for me means:

How might this fit within my wellbeing practice for everyday life?

What's something I'm excited to try, bring in or do?

INTEGRATING

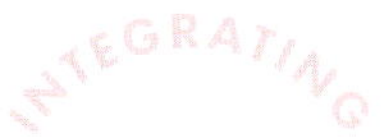

YOUR WELLBEING PRACTICE BUILDER

We're excited about where the next Pathway is going to take you. This one might need a complete refresh on how you approach it and often comes with a lot of weight (OK we realise we're stuck in pun world, and there's a hint here too of what we'll be looking at).

Until next time, we'll just be here hanging out together.

Don't forget to update your Pathway tracker on page 24.

- **GET OUTSIDE**
- **EMBRACE YOUR CREATIVITY**
- **INVEST IN YOUR RELATIONSHIPS**
- **MOVE FOR YOUR MIND**
- **ORIENT YOUR LIFE TO KIND**
- **LEAN INTO FUN**
- **RE-ENCHANT YOUR EVERYDAY LIFE**
- **LIVE WITH YOUR WHY**
- **EXPLORE WITH GRACE**
- **RE-EVALUATE YOUR LIFE WITH TECH**

LET'S PAUSE & REFLECT

REFLECTIONS

Let's take a minute to breathe and reflect on everything you've covered so far.

Over the previous pages you took a deeper look at the power of nature, explored what it can mean to lead a creative life and determined how important connection is.

As with anything, having this information and integrating it into our everyday lives are two separate matters. We urge you to be gentle with yourself as you move through this journal.

Instead of feeling inadequate because you haven't hiked Pen-y-Fan or overwhelmed because there is so much you 'should' be doing, we'd like to offer a paradigm shift.

The next time you are feeling off or overwhelmed, see if you can look to one of the Pathways you've covered and try to fold one of them into your life in some small way. Maybe that means gazing out your window for a few minutes, maybe it's scheduling a date with a friend or painting watercolours of pretty landscapes . . . whatever it is, we hope you use this information to benefit you and never as something to feel bad about.

Take a moment to reflect on what you've experienced so far and see if anything has shifted for you as you revisit where you were on day one. Go back to page 16 and just remind yourself why you're here.

As you practise some of these Pathways, note what's coming up for you.

Reminder: Why am I here?

I need to believe my wellbeing practice can:

Four goals I now have for my wellbeing practice:

What's working for me?

What's not working for me?

What would I like to change?

MORE FEEL-GOOD ACTIVITIES TO TRY

NATURE

YOUR CHALLENGE: GET OUTSIDE

PLANT AN INDOOR GARDEN
FIND THE BLUE (LAKES, SEAS, RIVERS, SKIES)
VISIT A PARK
PICK A BUNCH OF WILD FLOWERS (LEGALLY)
WATCH THE BIRDS

CREATIVITY

YOUR CHALLENGE: EMBRACE YOUR CREATIVITY

SPEND TIME WITH YOUR MOST CREATIVE FRIEND
CLEAR A SPACE IN YOUR HOME FOR CREATIVITY
START A DAILY JOURNAL
FIND INSPIRATION
DISCOVER HOW COLOUR MAKES YOU FEEL

CONNECTION

YOUR CHALLENGE: INVEST IN YOUR RELATIONSHIPS

SEEK OUT LOCAL PLACES
PARTICIPATE IN YOUR COMMUNITY
BE THE ONE TO REACH OUT FIRST
CHOOSE PEOPLE OVER APPS
JOIN ANY KIND OF BOOK CLUB

"If somewhere along the way you lost the part
of yourself that felt you could do anything, be
anything; if there is a part of you that doesn't
feel strong or doesn't know how to begin, that
doesn't feel you look the ways you 'should' or
feels ashamed in your own body, I am here
to tell you whatever you have believed in the
past does not have to determine your story."

– Poorna Bell –

RECONNECTING MIND & BODY

MIND & BODY

First, let's take a breath. You've been going deep on different aspects of your life. If you need a moment, here's your invitation to take one.

In this Pathway, it's all about getting embodied and exploring our Mind & Body connection, because we often seek to work on the mind when we're struggling, when it's the body that can unlock emotional roadblocks.

We'll be looking at how to be more open to working physically on the things you stumble on mentally. This sounds counter-intuitive, but we're learning that practices such as movement and breathwork can help us shift our thoughts, our emotions and our everyday lives.

If you read a book on wellbeing, this is the part you might have expected. So much of wellness leans this way, towards our bodies, how we're sleeping and what we're eating.

We need to bring this in because this is integral to how we function. But we wanted to offer you a reframe: to notice that the mind and the body are always in a relationship with each other. The mind and body have been traditionally separated, but now we're recognising the importance of rebalancing the connection and synergy between the two (they are nothing if not a mass of intertwined connections).

This Pathway helps you understand more about how the mind-body connection works, as well as focusing on movement and exercise as ways to connect with your emotional and mental wellbeing.

Of all the choices presented in this Pathway, we encourage you to find something that appeals to you. We've noticed in our research the wide variety of ways that people show up for themselves in this pathway: some turn to fly fishing, others to tap dancing. Different things work for different people, for different reasons. You may never like dipping into muddy rivers or competing in marathons, but you might happily run down sand dunes or dance to music. You may like to take gentle walks after school drop-offs or enjoy yoga while your child joins in. These are the things that make us happier; these are what works for our bodies and our minds.

This Pathway is about figuring out what works for you, playing around with different ways of moving, figuring out how you like to be in your body and becoming conscious of what's going on for you. We know that we feel best when we push ourselves in ways that fit with our goals, our personalities, our moods. Just be open to working physically on the things you stumble mentally on. Whatever it is that can help you de-stress and reconnect with yourself.

If for any reason you are unable to take part in this Pathway at this time or at all, then give yourself permission to skip it and move forward to the next one.

BENEFITS OF MIND & BODY

Research highlights how physical fitness supports mental wellness. Moving our bodies reduces stress, improves sleep, boosts mood, eases tension, enhances self-esteem and combats anxiety. Activities like walking release endorphins, the 'happy hormones' we all need. One caveat, recent research has detected 'an enjoyment gap', with fewer women reporting they enjoy physical exercise. To close this gap and help increase motivation, the report suggests finding exercise that is 'sociable, self-affirming, safe and suitable'.

Caring for our bodies is caring for our minds, yet in our busy lives this isn't always seen as a priority. Globally, a quarter of adults fall short of World Health Organization guidelines of at least 150-300 minutes of moderate-intensity aerobic physical activity per week, or 75-150 minutes of vigorous-intensity activity or an equivalent combination of both. How can you move more and enjoy these benefits? Let's find out.

DETERMINING WHERE YOU ARE

You may be completely disassociated from your body, someone who lives (happily) in their head. It's all about a life of the mind for you - you are a 'thinking person'. You might not even own a pair of trainers.

You may be curious to know more about the mind-body connection. Your interest is piqued, but you're not quite sure what to do with it. There's a slight concern it might involve dumbbells or 6 AM starts. That goes with a hope that it might help with life's inertia, with feeling emotionally leaden.

Or you are what some people call 'active', you might do triathlons for fun and need a burst of activity before you start your day. You fall more on the body side than the mind side. There is no start line. No 'and we're off' racing to some finishing point. This is about finding ways that work for you, in a realm that has something to do with both the mind and the body, that's as much about mental and emotional wellbeing as physical health. If there's any gym equipment present, it's a seesaw and we're playing with that balance and the pivot points to do with your mind-body throughout this month.

How did you rate yourself on the wheel on page 22 and now think about where you want to be? Take this into account as you move through the Pathway. Keep checking back if you need to.

Note where you are on the map below if this is helpful.

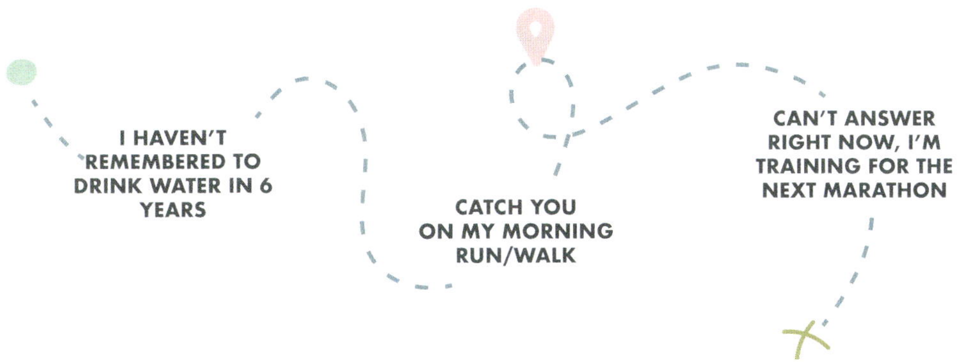

WHAT IS MIND-BODY FOR YOU?

The irony of this whole Pathway is there is quite a bit of mind work that needs to take place. Or you could go for a walk and complete these as voice notes. Let's explore (and attempt to unpack) what mind-body connection means for you, outside of societal pressures and expectations.

What does mind-body connection mean for you?

How is your body talking to you? How are you listening?

How can you start to tune into your body? Through meditation, through movement?

What would feel good to you?

List what movement activities give or have given you joy?

If you are not still doing them, what's getting in the way or preventing you?

List some movement activities you would like to try?

(Turn over the page for some inspiration if you need it.)

What's stopping you from trying something new and how could you approach this?

WAYS TO BE STILL

In this exercise you'll be finding one way you like to be still with your body and one way you might want to move it. Over two different days try each of these 5-minute grounding practices. Once you've decided which you prefer, do it each day for a couple of weeks. If you like them both then switch it up.

VISUALISE A SAFE SPACE

(Good if you need to remind your body of how safety and relaxation feel.)

Close your eyes and picture a place where you feel completely calm and at peace.

This could be a real location but it could also be an imaginary place.

As you visualise the details, what do you see, hear or feel there?
Spend a couple of moments immersing yourself in this space,
allowing it to soothe you. When you're ready open your eyes.

A BODY SCAN

(Good for remembering that we have a physical self and noticing sensations again.)

Close your eyes and take a few deep breaths, breathing in
through your nose and out through your mouth.

Now bring your attention to the top of your head, slowly moving your focus
down through your body. As you move from your forehead down to your feet,
notice any areas of both tension and comfort without trying to change them.

Acknowledge how each area feels and as you exhale allow yourself to
release any tension you are holding. Open your eyes when you're ready.

MOVEMENTS TO TRY

Need some more inspiration? Look at this checklist for movement and allow yourself to get curious about what an enjoyable movement practice could look like for you.

Mark the ones with a dot you'd like to try. Then mark with a tick once you've tried them and want to do it again. Mark with a cross any you don't want to do again.

<table>
<tr><td>☐ Dancing</td><td>☐ Swimming</td></tr>
<tr><td>☐ Walking</td><td>☐ Coasteering</td></tr>
<tr><td>☐ Hiking</td><td>☐ Orienteering</td></tr>
<tr><td>☐ Kayaking</td><td>☐ Tai Chi</td></tr>
<tr><td>☐ Climbing</td><td>☐ Qigong</td></tr>
<tr><td>☐ Paddle Boarding</td><td>☐ Zumba</td></tr>
<tr><td>☐ Surfing</td><td>☐ Boxing</td></tr>
<tr><td>☐ Sonic Bath</td><td>☐ Roller Skating</td></tr>
<tr><td>☐ Martial Arts</td><td>☐ Skateboarding</td></tr>
<tr><td>☐ Meditation</td><td>☐ Barre</td></tr>
<tr><td>☐ Skipping</td><td>☐ HIT or HIIT</td></tr>
<tr><td>☐ Breathwork</td><td>☐ Spinning</td></tr>
<tr><td>☐ Running</td><td>☐ Aerobics</td></tr>
<tr><td>☐ Cycling</td><td>☐ Kitchen Disco</td></tr>
<tr><td>☐ Pilates</td><td>☐ Rowing</td></tr>
<tr><td>☐ Yoga</td><td>☐ Trampolining</td></tr>
<tr><td>☐ Park Run</td><td>☐ Tap Dancing</td></tr>
</table>

Add your own here . . .

YOUR MINDSET SHIFT

MOVE FOR YOUR MIND

Now how can you think about movement differently, in terms of mental health and emotional wellbeing? You may have been conditioned to think about exercise in terms of weight loss and appearance, but what if we allowed space for it to be about feeling good in our minds and our lives?

How would you describe your current mindset about this Pathway?

What do you currently believe about this?

What do you need to change to shift this belief?

What learning is opening up for you?

What steps could you take, or experiences could you try to shift your mindset?

YOUR CHALLENGE

Reflect on your journal prompts and use them to explore how to move, slow down, try something new and deepen your understanding of the connection between your mind and body. Let these insights guide you toward curiosity about movement and what feels good for you. Think of movement not as a chore or an obligation, but as something you genuinely want to do. Your body is your home, and you deserve to feel comfortable, strong and at ease in it. Each week try something new . . . or keep something going.

- ☐ Try a new class.
- ☐ Take a walk in the park.
- ☐ Try a walking meditation.
- ☐ Choose a restful spot and just breathe.
- ☐ Go veggie or vegan for a day.
- ☐ Try all the sober-curious drinks in your local shop.
- ☐ Do something just for fun: rollerskating, surfing, ultimate frisbee.
- ☐ Stretch your capacity by joining a local challenge.
- ☐ Try one new physical activity.
- ☐ Notice three scents as you go about your day.
- ☐ Treat your body with a visit to a local wellness space.
- ☐ Add regular movement breaks to your day.
- ☐ Pair movement with an audiobook you love.
- ☐ Buy and use a skipping rope or hula hoop.
- ☐ Leave your car at home for the day.
- ☐ Find a way to walk and talk with a friend.
- ☐ Make an exercise playlist.
- ☐ Go on a bike ride.
- ☐ Vary things: different apps, trainers, YouTube.
- ☐ Make space at home to move, just enough to fit a yoga mat!

YOUR MIND-BODY PATHWAY

Hopefully you've gained an enhanced perspective on how your physical health supports your mental and emotional wellbeing. Before moving on, ask yourself: what are you committing to, and how will you know if it's working?

When we move for the sake of appearance, changes are visible. But when we move for our minds, to feel good inside, what will you notice? Less brain fog? More joy? Write down what will keep you motivated and how you'll redefine success on this Pathway. How can you make this your own? What steps will you take to integrate this into your life? Let's reintroduce experimentation and play as we move forward.

How might mind-body connection fit within your wellbeing practice for everyday life?

What's something you're excited to try, bring in, or do?

INTEGRATING

YOUR WELLBEING PRACTICE BUILDER

Next we're going to take you in a new direction. You'll be getting out of yourself and discovering one way to benefit your emotional and mental wellbeing that has very little to do with you at all. It's all about doing selfless good deeds and being kind.

Don't forget to update your Pathway tracker on page 24.

GET OUTSIDE

EMBRACE YOUR CREATIVITY

INVEST IN YOUR RELATIONSHIPS

MOVE FOR YOUR MIND

"There's a lot of evidence that one of
the best anti-anxiety medications
available is generosity."

– Adam Grant –

HARNESSING KINDNESS

KINDNESS

Welcome to the Kindness Pathway. Thank you for taking the time to work through this journal and for making space for yourself. In case no one ever tells you - you've got this, more than you know!

We've found that giving back to others doesn't often feature in a wellbeing plan. It doesn't come up when we're looking for a life less lonely, or for purpose in our lives, or for a remedy for all that life is throwing our way. Often, it's the add-on once everything else is settled.

But what if it's the place we start when we're thinking about how to feel better in our own lives? What if we made giving back fundamental to who we are and how we can think about our wellbeing in our everyday lives?

Over this Pathway, you'll look at the science of helping others and how we can shift our mindset from a focus on our individual lives to our collective wellbeing.

Giving back, getting outside of ourselves and supporting others have a positive impact on us too. Prioritising other people on our personal agendas helps us feel good.

We don't want to invite any idea of 'being better than others' into this Pathway. Giving back or 'doing good' can also be associated with 'being good', and there are a lot of nuances with this one. We know some incredibly kind people, who are struggling to get through the daily juggle, and don't currently have the capacity to volunteer at the moment. Those people are still 'good'.

So, let's be really careful here when we assess where you are. This does not determine your value; it merely indicates where and how you might wish to explore the concept of kindness.

Also, there can be a sense of doing all the 'giving back', we can burn out on contributing to community, supporting family and friends, going above and beyond at work. There can be self-sacrifice, even self-judgement around not doing enough, let's check that somewhere too. This is not to make you feel worse for not doing more of all the things; it's to make you access kindness in a way that is actually kind to you too.

Just know that kindness is not a weakness, it's not something decorative. Kindness can be a strength, it can be core to how we show up in the world. It involves both vulnerability and empathy, both powerful connectors (and still incredibly difficult places for us to step into). Kindness often comes with courage.

For some people, for this Pathway to resonate the most, they need to shift the language a little. From Giving Back to Doing Good. Or taking on an idea of service or that of activism. You might like the idea of changing the world, of volunteering or philanthropy, to help you identify more with an idea of care, compassion and support.

Find the words that excite you and capture how you would like this Pathway to work for you. Now let's take a moment to open your heart and discover how the profound benefits of kindness extend far beyond the simple act itself.

BENEFITS OF KINDNESS

Kindness might seem like a simple idea, but it has a powerful impact on our bodies and minds. Acts of kindness trigger the release of dopamine and serotonin, boosting our mood, calming the nervous system and promoting joy.

According to the Mental Health Foundation, kindness benefits both the giver and the receiver, increasing happiness and fostering social connection, though we often underestimate its effect.

Kindness reduces anxiety, combats depression and builds emotional resilience, contributing to a more fulfilling life. It's even contagious, spreading positivity to others. Just thinking about a kind act we did makes us slightly happier. Yet, when life feels overwhelming, we often retreat inward. So let's explore how small shifts toward kindness can make a big difference.

DETERMINING WHERE YOU ARE

You might already be acquainted with that wonderful feeling you get when you've helped someone, done right by the planet or contributed to your community. Or you may never look up from your life to notice there are ways that you could participate in the world around you that might help yourself as well as others.

Being of service, living a values-driven life, and working to end systemic inequalities might sound like things other people do, or conversely these could be the core of your very being right now.

This Pathway might exist just to help you see yourself as part of the bigger picture, the planet, society, your street. Or r it might be the catalyst you need to work on bettering something in your world, the environment, homelessness, racism or sexism. It could help you deepen a life already dedicated to the practice of doing good.

Wherever you are on this path, know that even small gestures are meaningful and that there are no comparisons to be had. There is space for all our actions, however big or small.

How did you rate yourself on the wheel on page 22 and now think about where you want to be? Take this into account as you move through the Pathway. Keep checking back if you need to.

Note where you are on the map below if this is helpful.

WHAT IS KINDNESS FOR YOU?

This Pathway might bring up some strong feelings and some even stronger assumptions, so let's see where you are:

What does kindness mean for you?

What are some of the beliefs you hold about this Pathway?

Which are you identifying with more: kindness, doing good or giving back?

What's a cause that matters to you?

What's in your capacity to give right now? (Time, money, learning, listening?)

Where does who you are (your strengths, experiences and values) meet what the world needs?

Note down a time you helped someone, how did it feel?

In what way did it impact your everyday wellbeing?

KINDNESS DIARY

According to Claudia Hammond, the writer of 'The Keys to Kindness', one of the best ways to start any kindness practice is to just notice kind acts around you, of people doing and receiving kindness. Note them in this journal. If it feels good to you, keep going beyond these pages.

MONDAY

TUESDAY

WEDNESDAY

THURSDAY

FRIDAY

SATURDAY

SUNDAY

GRATITUDE LETTER

Think of someone who makes you smile, helped you in some way, makes you feel good just thinking about or has had a positive impact on your life. Write them a letter to say thank you. Maybe even send it to them.

Dear

With gratitude,

YOUR MINDSET SHIFT

ORIENTATE YOUR LIFE TO KIND

Keep it simple. Orient your life to kindness. Notice the small gestures unfolding around you. Notice when you're offered kindness, celebrate yourself for extending kindness. You might find this harder than expected as we can live in a world that teaches us how to compete rather than collaborate, talk rather than listen and take rather than give. When making decisions over the next week, ask yourself: what's the kindest thing I can do?

How would you describe your current mindset about this Pathway?

What do you currently believe about this?

What do you need to change to shift this belief?

What learning is opening up for you?

What steps could you take, or experiences could you try to shift your mindset?

YOUR CHALLENGE

Try to keep in mind that studies have found that ideally we should perform multiple acts of kindness a day (known as kindness stacking) and vary what we do, to avoid hedonic adaptation, where we get used to what feels good. Similarly, acting from a place of pleasure rather than obligation and socially interacting (rather than just performing anonymous acts) helps us maximise the benefits of kindness to our health and happiness.

- [ ] Support your local animal rescue.
- [ ] Buy in bulk from a refill store.
- [ ] Find a way to be kind to yourself and repeat it.
- [ ] Borrow something you need rather than buying it.
- [ ] Bake double of something and give it away.
- [ ] Identify a cause you believe in and volunteer.
- [ ] Donate a can of something at your local collection point/food bank.
- [ ] Carry out a small act of kindness for someone.
- [ ] Pay for someone's drink/lunch.
- [ ] Find one way to help the vulnerable in your community.
- [ ] Identify a way to recycle, reduce, and reuse just one thing.
- [ ] Donate your time to a place that needs your help.
- [ ] Give your full attention to someone you care about.
- [ ] Compliment someone.
- [ ] Reach out to someone who may need to hear from you.
- [ ] Support local businesses rather than buying online.
- [ ] Share a skill that can benefit your local community.
- [ ] Sort your books and run a give-away coffee morning.
- [ ] Opt for sustainable clothes over fast fashion.
- [ ] Mentor someone.
- [ ] Clear your wardrobe and donate clothes to charity.
- [ ] Clear out unused toys or bric-a-brac and donate to a charity shop.

YOUR KINDNESS PATHWAY

What's started to come up for you in this Pathway? Is anything new resonating for you?

We hope you take what you've learned and use the information to start informing your everyday choices and habits. After all this is your unique life and your approach won't look like anyone else's.

Take a moment to note how, and whether, you build this Pathway into your plan for better mental and emotional wellbeing. Think about how being kind to others might help you feel better in your life.

How might this fit within your wellbeing practice for everyday life?

What's something you're excited to try, bring in, or do?

INTEGRATING

YOUR WELLBEING PRACTICE BUILDER

Five Pathways down and you're halfway through.

Next, we're going to lighten the mood a little, if things have felt weighty, and explore a whole other way of being in the world. This one might be the easiest and most fun Pathway for you and you might want to stay here forever. Or you might find your mind going to outings to the circus and you want to head for the exit. Let's see where this journal takes you next.

Don't forget to update your Pathway tracker on page 24.

- GET OUTSIDE
- EMBRACE YOUR CREATIVITY
- INVEST IN YOUR RELATIONSHIPS
- MOVE FOR YOUR MIND
- ORIENT YOUR LIFE TO KIND
- LEAN INTO FUN
- RE-ENCHANT YOUR EVERYDAY LIFE
- LIVE WITH YOUR WHY
- EXPLORE WITH GRACE
- RE-EVALUATE YOUR LIFE WITH TECH

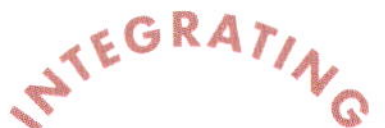

"This invitation to play is an invitation to get creative, to open up to new ideas, explore possibilities, find solutions. And it's giving you permission to do it without the pressure of finding the perfect next step."

– Eleanor Tweddell –

REMEMBERING PLAY & FUN

PLAY & FUN

Congratulations! You're either over halfway through this journal or maybe you're just flipping through the pages at random. Either way, we're so glad you're here! Along the way, you've been asked to do all sorts of things, from setting aside your scepticism and leaning into curiosity to getting excited about exploring where you live and getting crafty at your kitchen table.

Now, we're here asking you to do, perhaps, the hardest thing of all: have a little fun.

That's right, this Pathway is all about play!

You might be thinking this has gone too far. Being a grown-up in the world is no joke. There are bills to pay, dentist appointments to make, meetings to attend, meals to prepare and post to open. This stuff is real and pressing and can consume your time and impact your wellbeing. Believe us, we get it.

However, what if we looked at play as less of a denial of the seriousness of the world around us, and more as a means of helping ourselves to cope with it? Whilst play is often dismissed as frivolous, we've found it's often the opposite.

Some of us might have a knee-jerk reaction and dismiss play as something we did when we were younger. But research shows that it enhances overall wellbeing, increases resilience, boosts creativity and problem-solving skills, strengthens executive functioning, deepens connection, lowers cortisol levels, and even stimulates the growth of new neural pathways.

For example, have you ever seen someone look sad while throwing a frisbee? (Pretty sure it's not even possible.)

This Pathway is about suspending whatever disbelief you may have regarding the benefits of play and turning your attention instead to more important matters, like opening a board game, dancing in the rain or attending a comedy night with friends.

This Pathway is about letting it all go and finding that child within. Doing things that used to give you a lot of joy when you were young or finding something new that lifts the spirits and makes you smile and laugh.

Give it a go . . .

BENEFITS OF PLAY & FUN

As adults, we're facing near-constant pressure to produce, succeed and get ahead. We're planning and optimising and executing, cutting out anything that doesn't lead to a tangible outcome. For many, the concept of play is one we simply don't have time for. What if play actually helped us to grow our minds, become more proficient at work, deepened our connections and added some much-needed levity to our existence. According to research, that's exactly what it does.

Dr. Stuart Brown, founder of The National Institute For Play, believes that play is as essential to the human body as sleep. Throughout his book (Play: How It Shapes the Brain, Opens the Imagination and Invigorates the Soul) Brown reframes our basic understanding of play, stating "The opposite of play is not work, it's depression".

Research shows that adults who rate higher on playfulness scales (yes, this is a thing) are better able to reframe negative situations and that playful adults are more connected to their loved ones and their communities. Playing has the power to boost our creativity and aids in problem solving. Not that we're trying to focus on tangible outcomes here, but who doesn't love a little science to justify their fun?

DETERMINING WHERE YOU ARE

We can all probably think of a person who embodies this idea of play in adulthood. (They're the safety-risk flailing around in the bouncy castle at the children's birthday party.) Maybe we picture them laughing, or making paper planes, or turning some otherwise mundane task into an adventure. This is one version of play, and it can be amazing to see someone who has managed to hold on to this piece of themselves.

It's important to note that play is not one thing. It is not necessarily a loud or extroverted endeavour. Play can also be soft and quiet. It could be skimming stones across a stream, or looking up at the sky and making out shapes from the clouds, or having fun with a board game or two. Maybe it's sketching out make-believe characters for a book you've always dreamed of writing.

The wonderful thing about play is that there is simply no wrong way to do it. For this Pathway, your starting place is hardly relevant, because embodying play is less about where you fall on a spectrum, and more about how you're willing to shift your practices to do more, bringing more joy and connection to each day. We're not asking you to take up stand-up comedy, we're simply asking you to check in with where you are, and take one step further into the vulnerability of play.

How did you rate yourself on the wheel on page 22 and now think about where you want to be? Take this into account as you move through the Pathway. Keep checking back if you need to.

Note where you are on the map below if this is helpful.

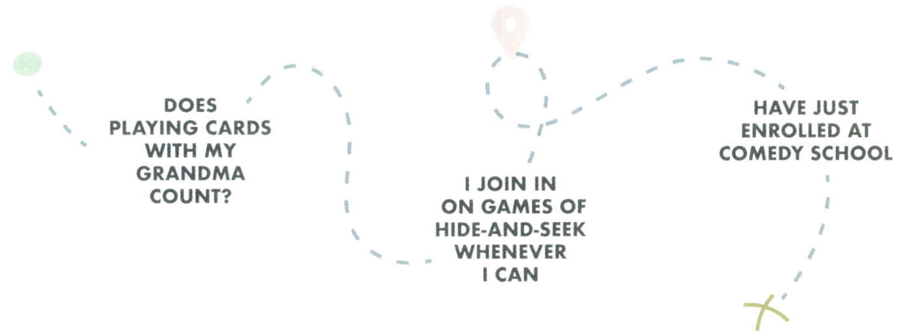

WHAT IS PLAY FOR YOU?

Use these questions to help determine where you find fun (and what might be stopping you from finding even more).

What comes to mind when you think of play & fun?

In what settings (and with who) do you feel like you're able to be playful?

What memories come to mind when you think of allowing play to unfold?

Which games or fun activities do or did you love the most?

Think of a time that play came naturally to you.

Is there anything holding you back from giving in to play?

How can you let play lead the way this week? Where might it take you?

EXPLORING PLAY

Dr. Stuart Brown, founder of NIFP, has dedicated much of his career to the study of human play: what it is, how it affects our health and the devastating consequences if it is suppressed. In his research he identified 3 distinct categories of play, each offering different outcomes. For this exercise, let's explore the 3 types of play and determine which areas you feel strongest in and which you might consider expanding into.

ROUGH AND TUMBLE

Rough and Tumble is about getting out of our minds and into our bodies. Whilst this may sound aggressive, rough and tumble play is actually rooted in joy and connection. (Think: dance parties, martial arts, football, etc.) To get started, think of some songs to create a playlist that gets your body moving:

IMAGINATIVE PLAY

Imaginative play, or pretend play, asks us to suspend reality and place ourselves in a make-believe world. Leaning into imaginative play unlocks our creativity, empathy and emotional flexibility, while also making us better problem-solvers and communicators. (Think: creative writing, art, theatre, themed parties, vision boarding and role-playing games). Who might you want to be for an hour or a day?

RITUAL PLAY

For some of us, rule-bound play is a safe haven from the wild west that are imaginative and rough-and-tumble play. Ritual activities are more structured activities that are often done in groups. (Think board games, escape rooms, card games and trivia nights.) What's your ideal games night?

We love a collaborative or group game, but sometimes a little solo activity is just the thing you need to get your brain moving into a more playful state. Try this playful word search challenge!

WHIMSY   FROLIC   TWIRL   FLUTTER   HAPPY

SCRIBBLE   SKIP   STARGAZE   DANCE   PLAY

A M P Y T U U B L E F Y A N P
I X X A U J W P G C Z Z L L A
W H I M S Y Y Q N N H R A L R
S D X T M J Z G F A B Y F H S
T Z S N W Y M L L D O Y T A A
U E K X S S U I W B Z T M P L
P L I O K T U D H K U L E P X
T B P X T A K E T L V E H Y S
H B Y E T R D P Q Z F R P S F
L I R V U G B K L R L N W M O
G R I J Q A J O O A X Z U Y W
N C H A U Z U L F D S T N Z B
T S Y B G E I T W I R L V M B
R O R Q Y C O S U W K X F T E

YOUR MINDSET SHIFT

LEAN INTO FUN

What would it mean to bring a sense of play to your life? Your brain might default to an idea of playgrounds and pillow fights, but play is going to take different forms for each of us. We have some ideas to inspire you on the next page. BTW: This one isn't for a boss, a friend or even a partner (although it's good to find fellow playmates to get silly with). This is entirely about what you intrinsically enjoy.

How would you describe your current mindset about this Pathway?

What do you currently believe about this?

What do you need to change to shift this belief?

What learning is opening up for you?

What steps could you take, or experiences could you try to shift your mindset?

YOUR CHALLENGE

Play can help connect us with more positive feelings. See if you can get in the habit of leaning into the fun of life and see where that joy takes you! According to the Broaden-and-Build Theory, popularised by social psychologist Dr. Barbara Frederickson, embracing positive emotions can spark a sort of upward spiral, enhancing brain function, boosting resilience and positively impacting our long-term wellbeing. So, the next time you're struck with a feeling of joy, lean into it and see where it takes you.

- [ ] Dig the board games out of the cupboard or buy some new ones.
- [ ] Visit an escape room.
- [ ] Sign up for an improvisation class.
- [ ] Initiate a game of hide and seek.
- [ ] Join a local, community sports team.
- [ ] Host a games night.
- [ ] Create a fantasy sports league.
- [ ] Write a poem.
- [ ] Learn a new card game.
- [ ] Talk in a silly voice to your pet.
- [ ] Play charades.
- [ ] Invite friends over for a themed dinner party.
- [ ] Have a spontaneous dance-party (alone or with friends).
- [ ] Make a balloon animal.
- [ ] Jump on a trampoline.
- [ ] Invent a game.
- [ ] Create a backstory for strangers in the cafe.
- [ ] Daydream about your future (be specific).
- [ ] Play frisbee at the park.
- [ ] Practise abstract painting.
- [ ] Attend a trivia night.

YOUR PLAY & FUN PATHWAY

There's something about play that can feel quite fleeting, like it's just a temporary add-in to our lives. But what if you made it into more of an anchor, something that you return to when you need a wellbeing reset? What would it take for play to become not indulgent but vital to how you care for yourself?

Over the previous pages, we hope that you've had a chance to experiment with play and maybe even found a way to return to the childhood joy it may once have offered you.

How might play show up in how you build your unique practice for your everyday life? Will it be something crucial to how you approach your days, or more of a footnote that you bring in occasionally? It's your way to well. How might you play with it?

How might you weave play into your everyday life?

What is something you're excited to try or do?

What is one way you think more play might benefit you?

INTEGRATING

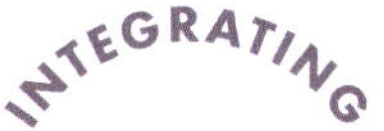

YOUR WELLBEING PRACTICE BUILDER

In this Pathway, you've been following a sense of play. In the next one, you'll be chasing wonder and discovering one of the most pro-social emotions. One that you might never have considered, but that could become your favourite and lead to your happy place.

In the spirit of being playful and before you start the next Pathway, there's now time to pause and reflect over the next couple of pages.

Don't forget to update your Pathway tracker on page 24.

GET OUTSIDE

EMBRACE YOUR CREATIVITY

INVEST IN YOUR RELATIONSHIPS

MOVE FOR YOUR MIND

ORIENT YOUR LIFE TO KIND

LEAN INTO FUN

RE-ENCHANT YOUR EVERYDAY LIFE

LIVE WITH YOUR WHY

EXPLORE WITH GRACE

RE-EVALUATE YOUR LIFE WITH TECH

LET'S PAUSE
& REFLECT

REVIEW

You're more than halfway through this journal. Well done!!! You've covered a lot of ground.

Let's take a moment to integrate what you've learned over the previous Pathways. You took a deeper look at what it means to form a positive mind-body connection, explored the incredible impact of kindness and dived deeper into your understanding of play and having fun.

Celebrate where you are. You're making changes and transforming who you are into who you want to be. There's also a lot we need to accept about ourselves; you do not need to change everything about yourself. If we bend and shape to someone else's perceptions or requirements then we will be left wanting when it doesn't work.

So today we want you to pause, and to acknowledge where you are feeling good, maybe even to congratulate yourself for what you are getting right.

As you explore these Pathways we're also hoping to highlight what works for you, allowing you to discover or rediscover where your happy place is. What enthrals you about your life right now? What captures your imagination? What are you proud of? In which Pathway do you shine? Take a moment to honour what's good today.

Your social conditioning might make this hard and your brain might also create some resistance. Your mind goes where it's always gone, it's kind of lazy that way, and its job is to keep you protected and safe. If your mind tends to see the negatives, it will take you there.

Sometimes bringing in the positives takes nudging and some perceptual re-framing. You may need to remind yourself often about where, or what, feels right to you. You can use your answers today to support that.

Overleaf is a reminder of where we've been. Catch up on what appeals to you. Create your own way through.

REFLECTIONS

What feels good to you? What's working for you?

In which Pathway do you shine?

What do you feel grateful for in your life at the moment? What positively impacts you?

What do you love, or even just appreciate about your journey so far?

FEEL-GOOD
ACTIVITIES TO TRY

GIVING BACK

YOUR CHALLENGE: ORIENTATE YOUR LIFE TO KIND

MAKE A POINT OF BEING KIND
SHOP SMALL, WHENEVER POSSIBLE
DONATE YOUR TIME/MONEY/KNOWLEDGE
KEEP A KINDNESS JOURNAL

PLAY & FUN

YOUR CHALLENGE: LEAN INTO FUN

BE REALLY SILLY
MAKE UP YOUR OWN GAME
DRESS UP FOR A DAY
HOST A MURDER MYSTERY DINNER PARTY

"The awe-inspiring, the numinous, is all
around us, all the time. It is transformed by
our deliberate attention. It becomes valuable
when we value it. It becomes meaningful
when we invest it with meaning. The magic
is of our own conjuring."

– Katherine May –

EMBRACING AWE & WONDER

AWE & WONDER

You may have noticed in this journal that we're trying to move away from a version of self-care that's solely individualistic to a form of collective connection and support. And this Pathway shows our interdependence more than most: it's awe. Dacher Keltner in his book 'Awe: The Transformative Power of Everyday Wonder' defines it as:

"Awe is the feeling of being in the presence of something vast that transcends your current understanding of the world."

When we experience awe, we often feel small (in a good way), and everything else (the to-do list, worries, obligations) falls away.

Experiencing feelings of awe is like pressing the reset button on our hectic lives, allowing us to momentarily step back and appreciate the beauty and vastness of the world around us.

Whether it's marvelling at the vastness of the universe or the kindness of strangers, these experiences remind us of the magic in the world and our place within it. Even when we briefly experience a sense of awe, we're more aware of how interrelated we all are and our sense of being separate leaves us. This leads to all kinds of prosocial and feel-good benefits: elevating our mood, reducing stress and even boosting our overall wellbeing.

Wonder, awe's softer cousin, sits naturally here: think of looking at the ocean, awe will be that feeling of being confronted with something vast, wonder will be reflecting on the wave patterns. It can be the quieter thing that opens our minds, creates a sense of fascination, feeds our curiosity and stretches our world. Often, we find this in the new, the novel and unexpected. Wonder allows us to learn and explore more of life in ways that are parallel and connected to awe.

For many of us, this can be hard; we're predisposed towards the knowable, the concrete, the realistic. We have undervalued our natural inclination for wonder. Maybe because it now feels flippant, even child-like. There's a risk that during this Pathway, our more cynical minds take over: "'You want me to make time to notice 'what exactly'? I don't have the capacity for that." It can feel incidental, rather than fundamental. Part of the wonder is to challenge these internal messages and train yourself to have more 'wow' moments.

By learning to reframe moments of awe and wonder, we will experience more moments of joy. Not only that, but we will also nourish our spirits and enrich our lives in countless ways.

In this Pathway, you'll be focusing on awe and wonder in your everyday life. From the small things - the flick of sunlight across a morning coffee, the courage a friend brings to a situation, the way the clouds move across the sky. To the big things, dolphins diving into the waves, how light shines just so to make rainbows after the rain. Where you find wonder, you might just find yourself again.

Awe and wonder can reside in vistas, but there's also a vastness that can be found in the subtle and ordinary, the overlooked or never seen.

What can you notice, where can you place your attention and what can you awaken to?

BENEFITS OF AWE & WONDER

Most of us can benefit from more awe and wonder in our lives. Though for you it may be called enchantment, mystery or the sublime. However you refer to it, awe offers a powerful antidote to daily challenges. Research by Dacher Keltner at Berkeley's Greater Good Science Centre highlights its broad benefits: fostering kindness, generosity and stronger social connections.

Experiencing awe and wonder also improves physical health, reducing inflammation, lowering stress hormones, improving cognitive functioning and increasing open-mindedness. They elevate mood and boosts life satisfaction and fulfilment.

In addition, by feeding curiosity and shifting focus from ourselves to the world, the benefits are felt not just by you but by everyone else.

DETERMINING WHERE YOU ARE

Did you notice how the light shone on that leaf a moment ago, or did you crumple it underfoot rushing for your train? Have you spent an afternoon wandering the galleries of a museum, or maybe you went straight to the coffee shop because the exhibition was a bit boring? Did that lecture/festival/bookshop inspire you to imagine more, or did you jettison the new possibilities they offered for more of the same? Did you gaze out of the window and notice the world on your train/bus journey or was your head down watching clips on social media?

For some, it is a sense of awe and wonder that we pursue through our days, curiosity seekers looking for the next jolt of recognition and connection. But for many, we don't build a practice of awe and wonder in quite the same way that we might take up a hobby, even though the way we navigate our days and walk through our lives can contain magic of all different kinds. What is your current level of awe-seeking?

How did you rate yourself on the wheel on page 22 and now think about where you want to be? Take this into account as you move through the Pathway. Keep checking back if you need to.

Note where you are on the map below if this is helpful.

WHAT IS AWE FOR YOU?

Is awe and wonder something you've considered before? Have you ever entertained the idea that embracing these experiences could enhance your overall wellbeing? If so, how do you seek out these moments?

What's your word for this Pathway that most resonates?

☐ Awe ☐ Enchantment

☐ Wonder ☐ Curiosity

Where do you find awe?

What settles your soul?

What causes it to awaken?

How would you like it to make you feel?

What diminishes your capacity for wonder?

Who do you know that has a sense of awe in their life?

What could you learn from them?

AWE DIARY EXERCISES

Awe can take different shapes in our lives. When Keltner asked people across 26 countries for their stories of awe, eight areas of life came up the most: nature, music, visual design, collective effervescence, spirituality, life, moral beauty and epiphanies.

You might experience awe in some of our Pathways like Nature (watching the ocean from the beach), Spirituality (standing in a sacred space), Creativity (being immersed in a particular piece of music or work of art), and Kindness (witnessing acts of compassion and courage).

You might find it in collective moments or effervescence (cheering on your team at a sports match or adding your voice to the cacophony at a concert). Sometimes it's encountering the big ideas and epiphanies that transform us (that feeling of 'ah, that's it', watching a Ted Talk). And it's even there in the cycle of life, our stories of birth and even loss.

Write down your moments of awe as you remember or experience them. Use this awe diary to capture these each week for a month.

More pages can be downloaded from www.fromyoutome.com/freebies.

YOUR MINDSET SHIFT

RE-ENCHANT YOUR EVERYDAY LIFE

We might think that awe holds no place in our everyday lives. That we have to travel to seek it out. Your challenge is to find the wonder where you are. To find awe in micro-doses in the places where you already exist. Could you find one thing that sparks awe each day? That could be as small, such as birdsong or the intricate patterns created by sunlight. Adopt a mindset of noticing the beauty in the everyday.

How would you describe your current mindset about this Pathway?

What do you currently believe about this?

What do you need to change to shift this belief?

What learning is opening up for you?

What steps could you take, or experiences could you try to shift your mindset?

YOUR CHALLENGE

To learn how to cultivate a greater sense of awe in your everyday life, you're going to open your mind and stretch your world by figuring out ways to identify and sustain wonder and feed your curiosity.

Threaded through this task are two ideas: the first involves shifting where you put your attention and the second is about becoming receptive to what's around you.

Pick those that appeal to you and try to fold these into your everyday life as you explore where - and what - awe could be for you.

- [ ] Learn how to name the constellations.
- [ ] Go small: notice 5 tiny wonders on a walk today.
- [ ] Go big: discover something that takes your breath away.
- [ ] Get to a place or viewpoint that makes you feel small.
- [ ] Find an environment that feeds your curiosity.
- [ ] Pay attention to the sights, sounds and smells of the natural world.
- [ ] Be a visitor in your hometown. Try to see it anew. Be a local tourist.
- [ ] Watch a sunrise or sunset.
- [ ] Do something that connects with a sense of child-like wonder.
- [ ] Listen to an inspiring audiobook or podcast.
- [ ] Join a citizen science project e.g. RSPB bird count.
- [ ] Take a course in something you want to learn and don't *need* to learn.
- [ ] Seek a local ideas-based lecture series or review a Ted Talk.
- [ ] Honour someone else's search for awe, giving them room to explore.
- [ ] Read an inspiring poem.
- [ ] Connect with animals (the ones in your life, the ones you can visit).
- [ ] Try an exhilarating new activity.
- [ ] Get philosophical and ponder life's big questions.
- [ ] Watch an uplifting documentary or a film about moral courage.

YOUR AWE PATHWAY

If we're open to it, the world is full of awe, and it can take us in many directions. For some people that will look like exploring the life of the planets, for others it's fictional worlds created in books. For some that means noticing the surprising in the mundane while on a local walk, for others making pilgrimages to sacred sites. For some, awe will be found in the quiet tale of someone overcoming adversity, others in a big idea shared on a stage in front of thousands. There are many ways to invite awe into your life. Where will you find it?

Awe is often forgotten when life gets in the way. Living at speed, looking down at our devices, allows no time to look all around. When we do look up and explore, there's a world of wonder just waiting for us to notice. Give yourself permission and the time to notice it.

How might awe fit within your wellbeing practice for everyday life?

What's something you're excited to try, bring in, or do each week?

How will you ensure you fit this in each day or each week?

YOUR WELLBEING PRACTICE BUILDER

Where this month has been about playing with your attention and enchanting your world, the next Pathway might feel different, because we're going to figure out something that may be core to you.

See if you can bring the same curiosity to that space too - it will help you navigate it better. As with awe & wonder, it's another Pathway that contains multitudes.

Don't forget to update your Pathway tracker on page 24.

"The good life consists in deriving happiness
by using your signature strengths every
day in the main realms of living. The
meaningful life adds one more component:
using these same strengths to forward
knowledge, power or goodness."

– Martin Seligman –

LOCATING PURPOSE

PURPOSE

You've arrived at the Purpose Pathway! Well done on getting this far? We're impressed that you've kept going, exploring your life from different perspectives and finding more of what matters to you.

Before we get into it, a quick note. We've found that Purpose can be a tricky one, and we've hesitated, because one of the things we're all now supposed to have is 'a purpose'. As if it's not enough to just be a person anymore. We recently heard the term 'purpose anxiety', the stress of having to live a life of significance. We're under pressure to live 'purpose-driven lives', to answer the most fundamental question, 'What am I here for?' In fact, the pressure of finding one's purpose can lead to increased anxiety and a greater negative effect on us.

There's some pushback too in that it can feel narcissistic (like "who am I to have a purpose", but also "I'm better than you because my purpose is more elevated"), based on ego rather than service, all inward stroking rather than supporting a life of engagement.

And there's some entanglements with outdated ideas of success and achievement, self-worth and striving, that we need to unpick here, that make the ideal of a purpose-driven life something that keeps us at our desks and living in narratives that resist any idea of rest for too long.

So why talk about it here? Living according to our purpose can give us clarity, be a filter through which we run our choices and reduce a sense of overwhelm by bringing clarity to how and where we spend our precious days. Having a purpose helps us feel more fulfilled, bringing confidence to how we show up in our lives. The search for purpose in and of itself can be meaningful, by allowing the space to learn, grow and explore with curiosity. Rather than seeing it as a fixed destination, see it as something dynamic: both the journey and the practice that adapts according to life stages and evolving

experiences. It does not have to be a marker in the ground that holds you in place, but a map that allows you to discover its contours within.

What does Purpose mean in the context of this Pathway? It's about the search for what is personally meaningful to you and that helps you engage with the world in some way beyond your self.

Purpose might be personal: the thing that gets you out of bed in the morning, the why behind how and where you spend your days, the underlying motivation and significance driving your actions, goals and interests. It might be communal, the intention for your contributions to a collective or workplace goal. Or it might be societal, the need that fuels you to contribute or change the world in some way.

Feeling fulfilled, feeling like our lives have significance. That's where purpose comes in. Our purpose can be the organising principle on which we design our lives, offering both guidance and direction.

So, there's clearly a dance we're doing here in this Pathway. Between looking for purpose while not beating ourselves up if we don't have one, believing we have the wrong one, or worrying that we haven't found it yet.

We need to avoid the pressure it might bring, while tapping into the direction it can offer. Want to tread that fine line and see where it takes you?

BENEFITS OF PURPOSE

Living according to our purpose has been shown to have many benefits including a longer life expectancy. Blue Zones are regions in the world with a high concentration of centenarians, people who live to be 100 years or older, and where people generally experience low rates of chronic disease. These areas share common lifestyle factors that contribute to their inhabitants' remarkable health and long lifespans. One of the contributing factors in these Blue Zones has been found to be a sense of purpose.

Having a greater sense of purpose in life has also been linked to greater resilience against stress, lower levels of depression and anxiety, improved immune function, and positive impacts on cognitive function. It's even been linked to a reduced risk of chronic conditions and premature mortality, helping us maintain healthy behaviours as we age.

When we're in flow, living these purposeful moments, we feel happier. Even our sleep improves, as does our overall wellbeing.

DETERMINING WHERE YOU ARE

This might be the Pathway that already consumes you. You live to work. You check emails on waking and the phone or laptop comes to bed at night. Your work moments are filled until they spill out into everything else: relationships, self-care, home, family. You have your purpose up front and clear and you are unwavering in your pursuit of it.

This might be the category that slightly terrifies you, the one you think you're supposed to have, the meaning and mission that comes with finding your life's purpose and spending your days in pursuit of it. You know, the thing that you are not doing now as you get yourself to a job that gives you a salary and nothing else. You feel like you are floundering.

You might find that some of this starts to tip into some other Pathways for you like Giving Back and Connection. That's OK, our life flows, and you'll find increasingly that these Pathways start to talk to each other; that conversation will just be very different for each of you. And as you navigate this Pathway, know that you are enough. This is about direction, it's about meaning; this exploration does not determine your self-worth. You are enough - always!

How did you rate yourself on the wheel on page 22 and now think about where you want to be? Take this into account as you move through the Pathway. Keep checking back if you need to.

Note where you are on the map below if this is helpful.

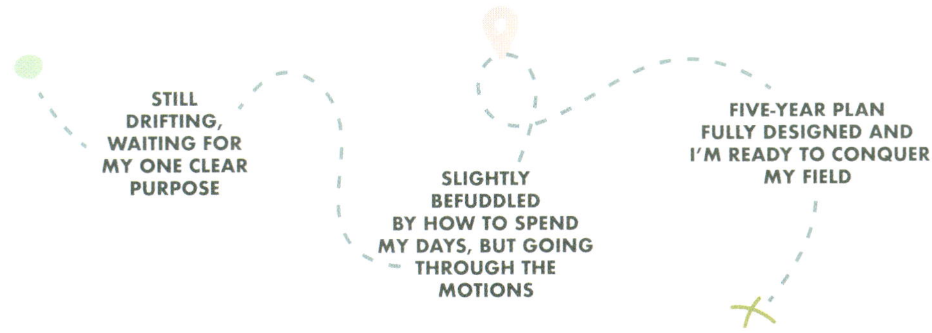

WHAT IS PURPOSE FOR YOU?

There are some deep questions throughout this journal, and this Pathway is possibly one of the most difficult for people to articulate.

We hope this Pathway offers some guidance for locating Purpose in ways that feel good to you.

What word for this Pathway resonates the most with you?

☐ Purpose   ☐ Passion

☐ Fulfilment   ☐ Motivation

Do you feel you have a sense of Purpose right now?

☐ Yes   ☐ No

Describe your purpose or reflect on a time when you were feeling purposeful. Where were you? Who were you with? What were you doing?

What feelings and thoughts come up when you think about having a purpose?

What's your motivation for finding a purpose? What would having a purpose do for you?

What would having a purpose expose you to? Are there any emotional risks?

What would a purpose open up for you? What would feel spacious about it?

What matters to you that you would like to allow more space for? What lights you up?

FINDING A FEELING OF IKIGAI

This self-coaching activity is designed to help you identify more of what matters to you. You may have heard of the term ikigai. It's a Japanese concept that roughly translates to "a reason for being" or "a reason to wake up in the morning". Finding one's ikigai is a dynamic process that leads to a deeply meaningful holistic approach to all of life.

Created by Francesc Miralles and Hector Garcia
(Which itself was originally created by Andrés Zuzunaga and adapted by Marc Winn)

The above diagram is based on a more western, career-oriented focus on ikigai, helping you identify your larger life aims and how to apply them in a professional context.

What do you love? Your passions, interests and the things that get you into a state of flow. This is all about what genuinely excites you.

What does the world need? The problems, challenges and needs that you observe around you. The places where you believe you can make a difference.

What are you good at? Your talents, skills, knowledge and experience. The strengths you bring to the world.

What can you be paid for? The skills, work, services and expertise that people would pay you for. The economic viability of spending time doing all the above.

FINDING YOUR VALUES

Look at the list of words below and consider the questions on page 142. Circle any words that resonate with these. Everyone's values are different; there's no judgment about which ones are 'good' and which are 'bad'. Which of these values do you need to discover your sense of purpose? Answer this from your position, not anyone else's. Approach this exercise with curiosity, self-compassion and acceptance.

Abundance	Conscientiousness	Health	Mastery	Safety
Accountability	Courage	Helping Others	Meaning	Security
Achievement	Creativity	Honesty	Mentorship	Self-Care
Activism	Curiosity	Honour	Moral Fulfilment	Self-Determination
Adventure	Dignity	Hope	Openness	Self-Expression
Aesthetics	Discipline	Home	Optimism	Self-Respect
Agency	Diversity	Humility	Passion	Sensuality
Altruism	Efficiency	Humour	Patience	Serenity
Ambition	Empathy	Imagination	Patriotism	Service
Animal Rights	Empowerment	Inclusion	Peace	Simplicity
Authenticity	Environment	Independence	Perseverance	Spirituality
Awe	Equality	Influence	Persistence	Spontaneity
Balance	Ethics	Initiative	Personal	Stability
Beauty	Excellence	Innovation	Expression	Stewardship
Belonging	Excitement	Inspiring Others	Personal Growth	Storytelling
Calmness	Exploration	Integrity	Perspective	Sustainability
Caring	Faith	Intelligence	Pleasure	Tolerance
Challenge	Family	Intimacy	Positivity	Tranquillity
Charity	Feminism	Intuition	Power	Trust
Citizenship	Forgiveness	Justice	Precision	Vulnerability
Clarity	Freedom	Kindness	Professionalism	Wealth
Collaboration	Friendship	Knowledge	Progression	Wisdom
Commitment	Fulfilment	Laughter	Protecting the	Wonder
Community	Generosity	Leadership	Environment	Workers' Rights
Compassion	Giving Back	Learning	Quality of Life	Workmanship
Competence	Global Awareness	Legacy	Recognition	Others:
Competition	Gratitude	Leisure	Reliability	
Confidence	Growth	Listening	Resilience	
Connection	Happiness	Love	Respect	
Contribution	Harmony	Loyalty	Risk-taking	

YOUR MINDSET SHIFT

LIVE WITH YOUR WHY

The author and inspirational speaker Simon Sinek talks about finding and living according to our why: the fundamental belief that drives everything we do. Get in the habit of asking yourself what your why is, making this an active inquiry in your life. Pay attention to what sparks something in your life and why that matters to you: maybe there's a pattern there?

If this brings a sense of uncertainty, take inspiration from the poet Rainer Maria Rilke and "live the questions", allowing yourself to be patient as your purpose unfolds.

How would you describe your current mindset about this Pathway?

What do you currently believe about this?

What do you need to change to shift this belief?

What learning is opening up for you?

What steps could you take, or experiences could you try to shift your mindset?

YOUR CHALLENGE

Know this: your purpose doesn't need to be something enormous. You don't have to save humanity; it could be small and equally as impactful, bringing generosity to your interactions with others, reducing your footprint on our planet, creating joy in your home. We often fail to see the value of micro-gestures, but those smaller movements spark magical ripples too, that go out into your life and those of others.

The search for purpose in and of itself can be something to ground you. It can allow for space to learn and grow, to explore with curiosity, to see what's available to you, and to live with possibilities.

- [ ] Be a mentor to someone local.
- [ ] Support the work of a local non-profit.
- [ ] Support local businesses or volunteer nearby.
- [ ] Learn a new skill from a local business/organisation.
- [ ] Connect with someone you admire.
- [ ] Be part of collective action.
- [ ] Find one way to reduce your daily carbon footprint.
- [ ] Sign up for a class for something you're curious about.
- [ ] Make your regular household items more sustainable and ethical.
- [ ] Attend a meet-up at your local co-working space.
- [ ] Find a conference and explore something that inspires you.
- [ ] Register for an online class.
- [ ] Identify one cause you believe in.
- [ ] Invite someone for coffee who you admire professionally.
- [ ] Write your personal social mission statement.
- [ ] Find one way to share your learning and expertise.
- [ ] Schedule in time to do nothing to avoid burning out.
- [ ] Try a strengths test to connect with your unique attributes.
- [ ] Do one thing this week that feeds a passion.
- [ ] Support a charity, in any way you can, for a year.

YOUR PURPOSE PATHWAY

If you take one thing away from this Pathway, let it be this: purposeful moments lead to purpose-driven lives.

Before we head to the next Pathway, let's take a moment to acknowledge something that often holds us back: fear.

Sometimes we know exactly what drives us, connects us, and where we want to focus our energy, but fear steps in. Fear of failure, uncertainty, or judgement can create barriers between us and our purpose. Pursuing what matters often requires risk-taking, vulnerability and challenging limiting beliefs.

While fear's role is to protect, it can overstep, keeping us small, hidden or stuck. So, what do you need to say to fear to move towards your purpose? Jot it down before we continue to the penultimate Pathway.

Hey fear, I need you to know . . .

What's something you're excited to try, bring in, or do?

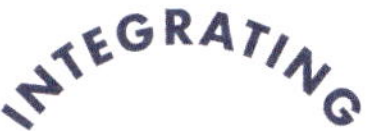

INTEGRATING YOUR WELLBEING PRACTICE BUILDER

We're actually going to stay in similar territory with our next Pathway, but this might feel even more intangible. For many of us though, this is where we derive most of our meaning. This Pathway might have been the background hum in your life, and we'll figure out how, and if, you foreground it. It's also your penultimate Pathway and you've made it so far. Keep going.

Don't forget to update your Pathway tracker on page 24.

GET OUTSIDE

EMBRACE YOUR CREATIVITY

INVEST IN YOUR RELATIONSHIPS

MOVE FOR YOUR MIND

ORIENT YOUR LIFE TO KIND

LEAN INTO FUN

RE-ENCHANT YOUR EVERYDAY LIFE

LIVE WITH YOUR WHY

EXPLORE WITH GRACE

RE-EVALUATE YOUR LIFE WITH TECH

"People of all ages, from all
backgrounds and in all walks of life,
are actively seeking a reconnection
to cycles, to nature, to understanding
rhythms, to receiving guidance and,
ultimately, a different way to live."

– Kirsty Gallagher –

SEEKING SPIRITUALITY

SPIRITUALITY

You've arrived at the penultimate Pathway. We're going deep and talking about spirituality and meaning (just...super light, right!).

While we don't know how you're approaching this Pathway, or from which direction, we'd venture to guess that, at some point in your life, you've experienced some form of spirituality.

Spirituality is about the fundamentally human search for deeper meaning by connecting with something larger than oneself, something transcendent, or even sacred. It's a broad concept that encompasses various practices and beliefs, and though it can be expressed as religion or faith, it can also be connected to broader experiences like mindfulness, being in nature, or compassionate acts. Spirituality takes us beyond the everyday mundane and our material lives to something less definable, the human spirit. This is soul work for the spiritually curious.

When we say spirituality and meaning, in this context we include: any belief system, ritual, gathering or process that helps you to orientate yourself in the world. This could be tarot as a system of self-care or a Sunday Assembly that grounds you in your life and community. It could be a meditation practice or the feeling of serenity that comes to you when entering a museum, bookshop, library or park. It's what it means for you.

For us, this is really about what feels bigger than you and yet helps you to understand your place, and maybe even meaning, in it all. For Amanda, the link between Spirituality and Nature is inextricable. For Claire, it is curiosity and awe that drive her explorations and understanding of something greater. Your challenge is to start to understand the type of connection you are looking for and the kind of meaning you need to bring sense to your world.

We realise that spirituality can, for some, be a very sensitive topic that can arouse strong opinions, intellectual arguments, and evoke thoughts of religion as opposed to value and belief systems.

In recent years, particularly among the younger generation, there has been a resurgence of interest in self-discovery systems like astrology, Human Design and the Enneagram, and exploring alternative practices like modern witchcraft, magic and crystals.

As we seek out alternative frameworks for understanding our inner and outer worlds and more easily accessible tools for self-care and reflection, where and how we choose to seek out spirituality might be more expansive than we previously thought.

If this Pathway feels a bit too much for you right now, please rest assured that you are free to answer these questions and contemplate these bigger concepts whenever you're called to do so. This is not something to put on a timetable or to-do list. It's something to explore when you're feeling receptive and open to all that can be.

So, moving forward, we ask just this: that you keep an open mind here. You allow any cynical inclinations to take a mini-break, and you offer yourself a moment to explore with curiosity.

BENEFITS OF SPIRITUALITY

We've been looking into the science of better emotional and mental wellbeing through this journal. Now that we're talking about spirituality, have we abandoned that completely? Are we inviting you to discard all rational thinking? Not at all.

In this Pathway, we're still coming back to research, and we've learned a few things that are significant: in 2022, the largest meta-analysis to date (David B. Yaden of Johns Hopkins University School of Medicine et al) found there was a positive association between religion/spirituality and life satisfaction.

Rituals can help reduce feelings of uncertainty and anxiety, with one study finding that a ritual in a local temple before speaking in public helped people feel less anxious than sitting and relaxing, while another found that even participating in arbitrary rituals in a lab was found to minimise the brain's response to performance errors. People who participated in mourning rituals reported lower levels of grief and an increased sense of self-control. In addition, participating in rituals and traditions (such as Christmas) has been found to strengthen relationships amongst family members, romantic relationships and adult friendships.

DETERMINING WHERE YOU ARE

This category can literally mean all or nothing to you. All being God, Gaia, Buddha, the Divine (really do insert the biggest thing you believe in here). Or believe in things, but not those kinds of things. You might think this is your northern star or the category that is least appealing to you.

But though at first it might feel like it's the most closed down, you know what you know and believe what you believe, it can also be the most searching. Across ancient wisdom and expansive viewpoints, through tarot, witchcraft, ritual, seasons, astrology, and on and on.

This Pathway aims to help you locate what can feel like the most ephemeral of things in ways that are meaningful to you (and it only has to be you, as this one can spiral into judgement all too quickly).

How did you rate yourself on the wheel on page 22 and now think about where you want to be? Take this into account as you move through the Pathway. Keep checking back if you need to.

Note where you are on the map below if this is helpful.

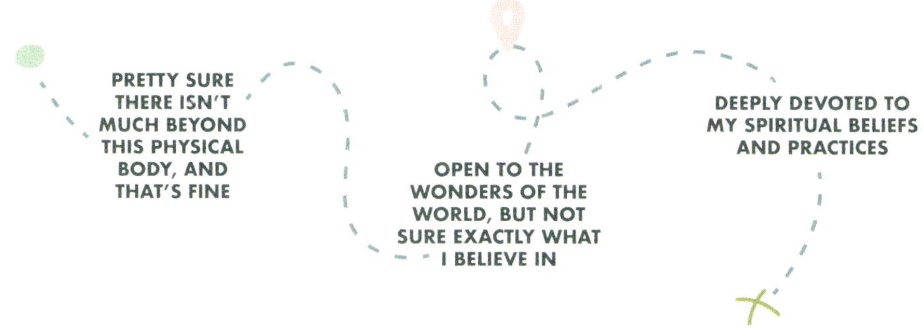

WHAT IS SPIRITUALITY FOR YOU?

We've asked you to reflect throughout this entire journal, and this is the one Pathway that opens the door to a space of contemplation, maybe more than all the others. As with our previous prompts, we've been tapping into your inner voice and your inner wisdom. Today we're going to be inviting in your inner serenity too.

Which words do you associate with Spirituality & Meaning?

What do you believe in?

What rituals matter to you in your life?
(Could be as simple as your morning coffee or how you celebrate birthdays.
Could be altars and dancing on the solstice.)

Which beliefs soothe you?

What 'rituals' do you have or want to bring into your life?
(Could be Taco Tuesday or dry January, Friendsgiving or Galentine's.)

What's your intuition telling you right now about something?

Where are the tiny flickers of light, the sparkles of magic, in your life?

CREATE YOUR OWN RITUAL

Design a ritual for your everyday life: a meaningful moment that you introduce into your day (or to make it even easier, you could bring more intention to an existing routine or habit).

Key components of rituals include creating a space and time to slow down, engaging your senses, focusing on the present moment and connecting with the intention.

- Light a candle at family dinner (and put away digital devices) to signal togetherness.
- Assemble a collection of meaningful objects to consider.
- Bring seasonal flowers or foliage into your home honouring the evolving year.
- Introduce a short meditation at bedtime to signal the shift from day to night.
- Write a daily script or scribble a couple of pages of reflection.

What is your ritual/what will you be doing?

What is your ritual designed to do? What is the intention behind it?

What time of day will you undertake your ritual?

SPIRITUALITY

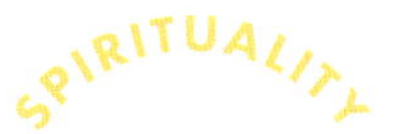

SOMETHING TO BELIEVE IN

Write a poem, a prayer or reflection. Somehow this form captures the intangibles of life, allowing us to see the magic of being. Write from the heart and soul and see where it takes you.

It could be about and/or to something you believe in.

It could be about or to whatever you hold sacred.

It could be about something that caught your attention this week and made you wonder what's behind it all.

It could just be about your cat, your best friend or a beloved tree.

YOUR MINDSET SHIFT

EXPLORE WITH GRACE

We're going to get spiritually curious. We've found that being cynical can dampen our curiosity. So, if you feel called, set cynicism aside and make some space to explore where we can make meaning. To look at what's available to you and see how (and always if) you want to integrate this into your life. To seek out meaning-making practices that fit with your values, your life.

How would you describe your current mindset about this Pathway?

What do you currently believe about this?

What do you need to change to shift this belief?

What learning is opening up for you?

What steps could you take, or experiences could you try to shift your mindset?

YOUR CHALLENGE

Reflect on your journal prompts and use them to explore how to find meaning, connect with something greater, and deepen your understanding of your spiritual and emotional self.

Let these insights guide you towards curiosity about what resonates with you and brings a greater sense of meaning.

- [ ] Read poetry, listen to a poetry podcast or attend a poetry reading.
- [ ] Attend a gathering that aligns with your beliefs and values.
- [ ] Seek out solace in a familiar ritual.
- [ ] Find a place that gives you a feeling of peace.
- [ ] Spend some time sitting quietly in a place that offers serenity.
- [ ] Seek out a place of wisdom.
- [ ] Try a new way of approaching the world . . . astrology, Enneagram.
- [ ] Gather friends around a new tradition, for example soup group.
- [ ] Light a candle for someone lost.
- [ ] Practice forgiveness by letting go of resentment around something.
- [ ] Read a text from a spiritual practitioner that soothes you.
- [ ] Create a sacred space in your home that feels grounding to you.
- [ ] Explore a different spiritual practice/philosophy for understanding
- [ ] Reflect on three things you are grateful for & note them down.
- [ ] Practice yoga/tai chi/Qigong to deepen your spiritual practice.
- [ ] Offer yourself some compassion today.
- [ ] Offer someone else compassion too.
- [ ] Learn where the meaning lives for you (ideas, gatherings, people).
- [ ] Find a quote that holds meaning for you and keep it somewhere close.
- [ ] Support (or even see) an elder in your community.

YOUR SPIRITUALITY PATHWAY

What's fascinating to us about this Pathway is how many of us are now shaping our own personal belief systems, drawing widely from different ways of approaching the world, ancient spiritual practices that can help us make sense of uncertain times and make sense of ourselves. We look to them for the stories they can tell us, for the mirrors they hold up for us, for the directions they might hint at. What role did you discover that spirituality or a meaning-making practice can play in your wellbeing?

What do you feel drawn to?

What learnings do you want to note here about what you need?

YOUR WELLBEING PRACTICE BUILDER

For the last Pathway, you're going to pull away from one of the places you probably currently seek out most often, like on average 150 times per day, even though (and you know this already) it's not really helping you.

What could that be? It's also our last Pathway so let's untether . . .

Don't forget to update your Pathway tracker on page 24.

GET OUTSIDE

EMBRACE YOUR CREATIVITY

INVEST IN YOUR RELATIONSHIPS

MOVE FOR YOUR MIND

ORIENT YOUR LIFE TO KIND

LEAN INTO FUN

RE-ENCHANT YOUR EVERYDAY LIFE

LIVE WITH YOUR WHY

EXPLORE WITH GRACE

RE-EVALUATE YOUR LIFE WITH TECH

"In a world crowded by the white
noise of other people's narratives – the
collective narrative of social media;
the multi-strand narratives of binge-
TV – having your own, singular, internal
narrative is nothing short of essential."

– Pandora Sykes –

LEARNING TO UNTETHER FROM TECH

UNTETHERING

We've looked at the health of our souls with an aim to re-charge them. In this last Pathway, we're going to be looking at something that might be draining them, the ultimate un-maker of meaning, tech.

Our phones, social media accounts, apps and laptops give shape to our days, our friendships, even our sense of self. But, as with all relationships, we need to find a healthy balance and happy boundaries to make tech work for us.

The irony is not lost on us that for many of us we now manage or support our everyday wellbeing through tech. We come together in online communities, we may meditate via an app, we're pinged by our phones and communicated with via text, email and social posts.

When was the last time you called someone rather than messaged them? Or worried about not getting the daily bonus from your apps? When 'likes' from strangers are more important than positive interactions with our friends and newsreels at the start of the day define our mood rather than what's ahead of us, then something might just be tipping the wrong way.

So why do we do it? Using technology can trigger a release of dopamine, often described as a 'dopamine hit', which is a neurochemical response associated with pleasure and reward. This can lead to a cycle where individuals seek out more of the stimulating activity, potentially contributing to problematic tech overuse.

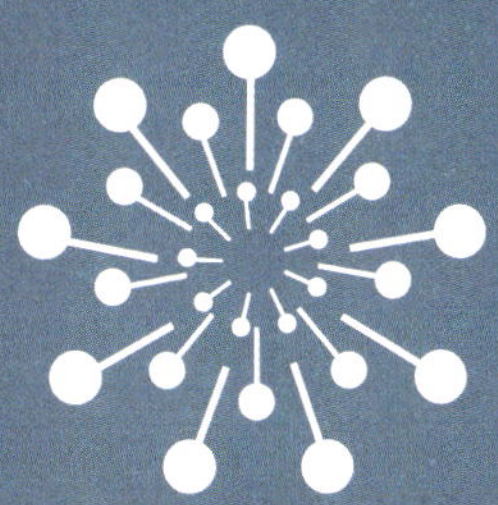

We might also find that we're tethered to tech because it fulfils a fundamental need: that of belonging. One study out of McGill University, Montreal explored how it is tech's prosocial nature that keeps us connecting and showing up in online spaces. Do you ever find that you've lost time just scrolling through endless unnecessary video clips?

It's a balancing act. The key lies in mindful usage and striking a balance between the benefits and potential risks. Promoting digital literacy, encouraging healthy online habits, and prioritising offline activities are essential for maximising the positive effects of technology while mitigating its potential harm.

We live in an era when AI (Artificial Intelligence) is racing into our lives, and the implications of that are yet to be fully understood, but it's still part of tech so the impact will most likely be relevant as we become more reliant on it.

Should you really throw your cell phone in the river? Probably not, but maybe you can leave it at home (heart racing!!!???). There are less drastic ways to untether.

So we're going to be working to heal your relationship with tech. We'll be figuring out how you might be self-soothing with your phone (for some of us they've become grown-up attachment objects), how we might catch that wandering brain of yours, and how you can better exist online and off.

BENEFITS OF UNTETHERING

Technology's impact on wellbeing is multifaceted. There are benefits such as fostering connection (making it easier than ever to find our people), providing instant access to information, and enabling us to engage in activities studies call 'attractive leisure'.

But when it tips too far, and it often does, we're on a downward spiral. Research also indicates that the use of tech gadgets and social media can impact face-to-face interactions and increase social isolation. While studies show that "problematic smartphone use" can be linked to anxiety, depression, sleep disruption and reduced physical activity.

Tech overuse even negatively impacts our physical health through lack of physical activity (isn't it so much easier to spend an hour watching fast paced reels than it is to spend an hour doing exercise). It also increases cognitive load, shortens attention spans, raises stress and leads to overconsumption, of both products and negative news.

And you might have experienced first-hand how social media fuels discord, inflames outrage, and reduces the quality of our interactions.

DETERMINING WHERE YOU ARE

Let's first establish where you are in relation to this Pathway, and what you are bringing as you arrive here. Is your phone your life? Not only containing your life, all those passwords and banking app transactions, that's how you run your life! It's how you spend your days, looking down, scrolling through, liking and clicking, commenting and messaging. Or are you clutching onto the analogue, book in hand, silent retreat booked?

Maybe you are someone who needs the connection that comes with being instantly available, who finds untethering unsettling and needs to know they are not missing out. Or perhaps you are someone who is burned out on checking, checking, checking, who feels tied down rather than as refreshed as the pages demanding your attention.

Tech is embedded into our lives: it's how we connect, play, work and learn. This Pathway will help you to acknowledge that you can choose how it shows up and when you would like it to demand your attention.

In this Pathway, you'll be working towards intentional device use and an active relationship with tech, both of which will support better mental and emotional wellbeing in your everyday life.

How did you rate yourself on the wheel on page 22 and now think about where you want to be? Take this into account as you move through the Pathway. Keep checking back if you need to.

Note where you are on the map below if this is helpful.

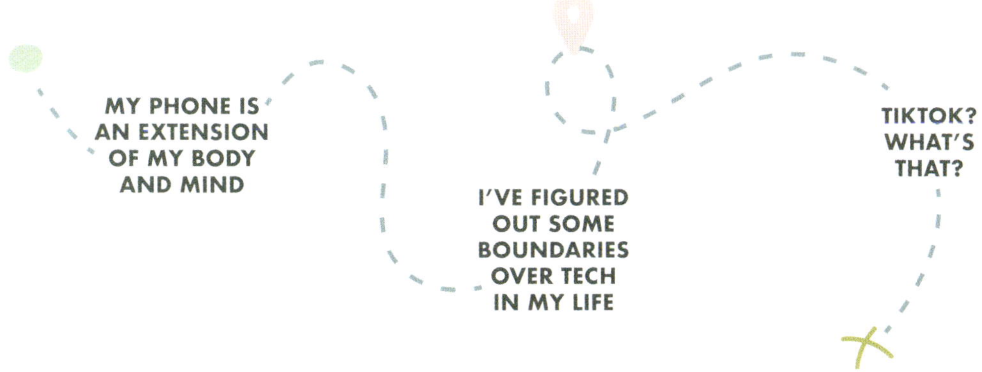

WHAT IS UNTETHERING FOR YOU?

For these journal prompts what we're really looking for is any increased self-awareness for improved self-regulation. Be honest with yourself here. Knowing where you truly are with tech can lead to a healthier, positive, intentional, sustainable and feel-good relationship with your devices, even if in the moment what you might discover feels a little uncomfortable.

What tech do you use and when . . .

How does technology take you away from things you want to be doing?

What thoughts arise when you think about removing tech? For an hour? For a day? Longer?

What does tech give you? How might it benefit you?

List the apps that are on your phone and how they make you feel:

Which ones will you shift away from or delete?

BREAKING THE CYCLE

When you reach for your phone what's the feeling you're avoiding or distracting yourself from? Before you pick up tech, know why, then find something else to do.

Tick which apply:

☐ Sadness

☐ Boredom

☐ Loneliness

☐ Other

What would you prefer? Tick which apply:

☐ Connection

☐ Belonging

☐ Humour/Joy

☐ Other

BREAKING UP WITH YOUR PHONE

Record how much time you spend on your phone.

Note: pick a typical week and note the length of time below

Monday	Tuesday	Wednesday	Thursday	Friday	Saturday	Sunday

Cover up this vase of flowers with your phone. Now go and do something else (non tech).

What did you do? How did this feel? What did you notice? How long did you last?

YOUR MINDSET SHIFT

How would you describe your current mindset about this Pathway?

What do you currently believe about this?

What do you need to change to shift this belief?

What learning is opening up for you?

What steps could you take, or experiences could you try to shift your mindset?

YOUR CHALLENGE

By stepping away from screens, you'll create space to explore what brings meaning, balance, and a deeper sense of purpose to your days. Let this be an invitation to pause, reflect, and rediscover the world beyond the digital.

- [ ] Download an app where you can restrict the times you use tech.
- [ ] Turn off notifications or set times each day when they are turned off.
- [ ] Leave your phone at home when you go out for a walk.
- [ ] Set times when you don't use your phone e.g. when you are eating.
- [ ] Turn off your phone and go cold turkey for 24 hours.
- [ ] Set time limits on your phone particularly for non productive apps.
- [ ] Invest in an alarm clock & keep your phone out of your bedroom.
- [ ] Turn on grey scale (it's horrible).
- [ ] Have a set place to charge your devices (not where you sleep).
- [ ] Need something in your hand? Stop scrolling and buy a physical book.
- [ ] Unfollow any accounts that give you negative feelings.
- [ ] Talk to the people you live with.
- [ ] Resist posting your digital detox on social media.
- [ ] Schedule phone/social media/tech-free days.
- [ ] Take a weekend/unplugged mini break away from it all.
- [ ] Find an accountability partner to 'untech' with.
- [ ] Protect your non-screen time like it's a gift to yourself.
- [ ] Sleep instead of scroll (often it's sleep that takes the hit).
- [ ] Exercise without using a health tracker.
- [ ] Buy a camera and ditch the one on your phone.
- [ ] Use a recipe book and bake something you've never made before.
- [ ] Learn how to knit or crochet (pick this up instead of your phone).
- [ ] Do a big jigsaw.

YOUR UNTETHERING PATHWAY

Can you believe that you are here? On the last Pathway? We're so, so proud of you and grateful you chose to spend your time completing this journal no matter how long it took you.

In the next section, you'll be wrapping all of this up so that you'll come away with your tailored practice for everyday life. Something that you can return to again and again.

You have taken this time to create the foundations for living your life in a way that can truly work for you and support you to have more good times. Before you move on let's wrap up with the last questions . . .

How might untethering fit within your wellbeing practice for everyday life?

What's something you're excited to try?

YOUR WELLBEING PRACTICE BUILDER

Over the past ten Pathways you've allowed yourself to explore wellbeing in a multitude of ways. You've built your unique approach to wellbeing as you've done so. You're about to discover how to bring it all together. We're excited to see where all these learnings and experiments, epiphanies and soul-searching, take you. Let's find out.

Turn the page to choose the most 'you' of wellbeing adventures.

Don't forget to update your Pathway tracker on page 24.

GET OUTSIDE

EMBRACE YOUR CREATIVITY

INVEST IN YOUR RELATIONSHIPS

MOVE FOR YOUR MIND

ORIENT YOUR LIFE TO KIND

LEAN INTO FUN

RE-ENCHANT YOUR EVERYDAY LIFE

LIVE WITH YOUR WHY

EXPLORE WITH GRACE

RE-EVALUATE YOUR LIFE WITH TECH

MORE FEEL-GOOD ACTIVITIES TO TRY

AWE & WONDER
YOUR CHALLENGE: RE-ENCHANT YOUR EVERYDAY LIFE

TAKE AN AWE WALK
CREATE YOUR OWN AWE RETREAT AT HOME
SEEK OUT HOLDERS OF AWE
ALLOW YOURSELF TO GET LOST

PURPOSE
YOUR CHALLENGE: LIVE WITH YOUR WHY

DISCOVER YOUR STRENGTHS
CONNECT WITH YOUR FUTURE SELF
UNDERSTAND YOUR IKIGAI
BE OK WITH NOT HAVING A TRADITIONAL "PURPOSE"

SPIRITUALITY & MEANING
YOUR CHALLENGE: EXPLORE WITH GRACE

FIND A WAY TO ORIENTATE YOURSELF
LOCATE YOUR SANCTUARY
END YOUR DAY WITH GRATITUDE
RECONNECT TO WHERE YOU ARE

UNTETHERING
YOUR CHALLENGE: RE-EVALUATE YOUR RELATIONSHIP WITH TECH

TAKE A BREAK
USE TECH MORE HUMANELY
FEEL THE FEELINGS
PAY ATTENTION TO WHAT YOU CONSUME
LIVE THE ANALOGUE

It's almost time to celebrate . . .
you've made it through all the Pathways!

But there is still a little more to do. Flip the page to check it out.

"Always end with the
beginning in mind."

– Todd Henry –

DEFINING A WAY FORWARD

DEFINING A WAY FORWARD

Over the course of this journal, you've been learning how to be in your life.

You've given yourself a moment to review all that you may need to build a happier life and then put it into place.

You've asked yourself some of the biggest questions, including maybe one of the biggest: how do we find the path to ourselves?

Some of this has been about unlearning, rewinding back some things we've been sold by the culture at large (or our families of origin, our schools, etc.). Much of this has been exploring, as you've learned resources, practices and tools to help situate yourself in your everyday life.

Together we've worked to discover what better emotional and mental (as well as physical, spiritual, social and digital) wellbeing is for you and determined where the imbalances in your life might be. By looking at the ten Pathways you now have an overview of how the things that are vital to your own wellbeing are showing up in your life, or maybe even where they are lacking. Now it's time to create an actionable plan for moving forward.

You have one final set of exercises to pull it all together. By the end of this journal, you'll have in your hand your personalised wellbeing practice, your very own feel-better prescription/blueprint/toolkit for everyday life, and the scaffolding for living more of what matters to you.

Let's make sure you are noting where you're most comfortable, expanding when you are ready, and gently nurturing aspects of living you might have overlooked. Review the ten Pathways, and your notes in this journal. Now look to identify:

1. One Pathway you felt good in:

2. One Pathway you want to further stretch into:

3. One Pathway that's been neglected and you want to revive:

These answers will form the basis for your wellbeing plan (page 186) and you can copy them over. The reason for the date is so that you can redo this exercise every month, making this your monthly practice. Downloads to help you with can be found at www.fromyoutome.com/freebies

DEFINING A WAY FORWARD

Starting in an area where you're already comfortable is a great place to begin. Maybe you already have a spiritual practice or a habit of getting into nature. Whatever it is that you already do that feels good, start there. Note one Pathway where you are already comfortable, and you want to maintain.

PATHWAY   **DATE**

How do you feel about
where you are?

What would you like to
keep most about this?

Where would you ideally like to be?

Now what's one step you can
take in that direction?

The second area of focus is the Pathway you'd like to develop a bit more. Note one area you'd like to stretch into more fully, a path that might be a challenge, but one that you're up for tackling.

PATHWAY   **DATE**

How do you feel about where you are?

What would you like to change most about this?

Where would you ideally like to be?

Now what's one step you can take in that direction?

DEFINING A WAY FORWARD

Finally, let's address an area you may be having difficulty with, so choose one Pathway that has been neglected or that you feel something is lacking.

PATHWAY   **DATE**

How do you feel about where you are?

What would you like to change most about this?

Where would you ideally like to be?

Now what's one step you can take in that direction?

On the next page you will get creative. Draw yourself (stretch that Creative Pathway) at the centre of the page or add a small photo. Then add in each of the ten Pathways in any way, any size and anywhere you want to demonstrate how integral to your wellbeing practice they are.

Once you have done that, fill in the fields around the side of the page. This will be your blueprint for better everyday wellbeing. Perhaps photocopy it and place it on your fridge. Here is an example:

EVERYDAY WELLBEING GOALS

GO OUTSIDE   SPEND TIME WITH PEOPLE I LOVE

MAKE SOMETHING   MEDITATE

MY WELLBEING VALUES

JOY

BALANCE

ADVENTURE

VULNERABILITY

PEACE

FUN

BELIEFS THAT FEEL GOOD

GOOD THINGS ARE ALWAYS HAPPENING

PERFECTION DOES NOT EXIST

EVERYTHING IS TEMPORARY

FEELINGS I WANT TO INVITE IN

OPTIMISM   CREATIVITY   HOPE

PEACE   PLAYFULNESS

EVERYDAY WELLBEING GOALS

**MY WELLBEING
VALUES**

**BELIEFS THAT
FEEL GOOD**

FEELINGS I WANT TO INVITE IN

Write down anything else you'd like to capture:

Now you've got your bespoke everyday wellbeing practice in hand, let's just check in about what might get in the way.

What might get in the way of me continuing with my wellbeing practice?

What will I do to reduce these barriers?

How will I stay committed to my plan?

How will I know if this is working for me?

What might be awakening in me?

Where am I finding the flow of my life?

I've come this far, how do I want to continue my journey?

YOU DID IT!

You've made it through this journal! That's a huge accomplishment.

Your path is your own, now where will it take you? We wish you curiosity, acceptance and joy as you step forwards.

We trust you've enjoyed exploring the Pathways. Just remember that you can return to them again whenever you choose. You may have found that there are some you leaned towards, others that you wanted to lean away from, but we encourage you to keep exploring them as we believe over time this will change. We hope that the work you've done promotes good days, and there are resources you can turn to for support, inspiration and encouragement.

We hope you've uncovered something about who you are and how you're showing up in the world, learned how to fully inhabit your life and restored intentionality to your everyday life choices.

Above all, we hope you've rediscovered your inner wisdom: what you've really been learning is how to connect with you.

We want to tell you that you're all set now. That you've arrived at some ending, your work here is done. We want to tell you that you've gone from A to B and now here you are, all finished. But we don't believe that. And we're sure you don't either. If the exercises in this journal have shown you anything, we hope that it is this: there is no endpoint, there is only curiosity and movement and trying. It's the reason they are called Pathways, because we all need to keep travelling along them.

This is foundational work that can help you for a lifetime. You can return to it again and again. You've identified practices that align with your values, beliefs and strengths, you now know where your boundaries are, and you have a sense of where you can connect with what matters most.

Remember, you can always revisit this journal's prompts, inspiration and encouragement when you need it. These practices are for life.

Note to self: accept that you may step off, because all you have to do is step back on.

As an ongoing ritual, see if you can revisit your answers each month to determine what has worked for you and what hasn't. Or even start again and see what's new for you.

This journal is designed to help you orient yourself wherever you are, to seek and find, and then allow yourself to maybe seek and find again, and again, and then again. Because that is what life is. That is the practice, ceaseless, unending, and entirely of your own making.

Now, it's time to take what you've learned and start living it out. How will you wander in your everyday life?

It's time for you to head off, into the world, armed with some new information about who you are and what you need. Don't forget to update your Pathway tracker on page 24.

We're excited to see where this takes you. We hope you are too.

THANK YOU!

Thank you for spending time working through this journal. We know how hard it can be to find the time to do all the things that need doing, so we're grateful that you chose to spend some of your moments with us.

Over this journal, you've worked your way through:

- 10 Pathways,
- 190 pages of journal prompts
- Self-coaching activities
- And many challenges

All in order to create a practice for better emotional, mental, social, spiritual and physical wellbeing in your life

We hope you'll keep in touch on social media via our Instagram account **ifloststarthere** where you can get more information, access to podcasts and more. Our website is www.ifloststarthere.com

Now go live that life of yours in all the joyous ways it can offer you.

Love,

Claire & Amanda

REFERENCES

NATURE

Nisbet EK, Zelenski JM. (2011). *Underestimating nearby nature: affective forecasting errors obscure the happy path to sustainability.* Psychological Science, 22(9), 1101–1106.
https://doi.org/10.1177/0956797611418527

This study found that people make affective forecasting errors about spending time in nature by underestimating positive emotional benefits.

Shuda, Q., Bougoulias, M., & Kass, R. (2020). *Effect of Nature Exposure on Perceived and Physiologic Stress: A Systematic Review.* Complementary Therapies in Medicine, 53, 102514.
https://doi.org/10.1016/j.ctim.2020.102514

This systematic review was designed to evaluate how nature can impact stress levels, both perceived and physiological. It found that nature has a positive effect in reducing stress, across both measures.

Weinstein, N., Przybylski, A. K., & Ryan, R. M. (2009). *Can Nature Make Us More Caring? Effects of Immersion in Nature on Intrinsic Aspirations and Generosity.* Personality and Social Psychology Bulletin, 35(10), 1315–1329. https://doi.org/10.1177/0146167209341649

Exploring whether nature can make us more caring, across four studies the authors found that being in nature lowered extrinsic aspirations (the long-term values that guide our lives) and increased intrinsic ones.

Berman MG, Jonides J, Kaplan S. *The cognitive benefits of interacting with nature.* Psychological Science, 19(12), 1207–1212.
https://doi.org/10.1111/j.1467-9280.2008.02225.x

This study compared how natural versus urban environments can impact the quality of our attention, finding that the former had restorative benefits for our cognitive function.

Bratman, G. N., Daily, G. C., Levy, B. J., & Gross, J. J. (2015). *The benefits of nature experience: Improved affect and cognition, Landscape and Urban Planning,* 138, 41-50.
https://doi.org/10.1016/j.landurbplan.2015.02.005

This study found that exposure to greenspace positively impacts cognition (increased working memory performance) and affect (i.e. anxiety and rumination).

Menhas, R., Yang, L., Saqib, Z. A., Younas, M., & Saeed, M. M. (2024). *Does nature-based social prescription improve mental health outcomes? A systematic review and meta-analysis,* Frontiers in Public Health, Volume 12.
https://doi.org/10.3389/fpubh.2024.1228271

This meta-analysis attests to the effectiveness of nature-based social prescription (NBSP), suggesting that they can complement traditional therapies and improve mental health outcomes

Jimenez, M. P., DeVille, N. V., Elliott, E. G., Schiff, J. E., Wilt, G. E., Hart, J. E., & James, P. (2021). *Associations between nature exposure and health: A review of the evidence.* International Journal of Environmental Research and Public Health, 18(9), 4790.
https://doi.org/10.3390/ijerph18094790

This narrative review of the recent (last ten years) experimental and observational studies on nature and health found a wide range of positive benefits from improved cognitive function to increased levels of physical activity.

Meredith, G. R., Rakow, D. A., Eldermire, E. R. B., Madsen, C. G., Shelley, S. P., & Sachs, N. A. (2020). *Minimum time dose in nature to positively impact the mental health of college-aged students, and how to measure it: A scoping review.* Frontiers in Psychology, 10, 2942.
https://doi.org/10.3389/fpsyg.2019.02942

A scoping review that aimed to establish the ideal nature-dose for college-aged students and found that just 10 minutes of sitting or walking in nature-based settings had a significant and positive impact on psychological and physiological wellbeing

Hunter, M. R., Gillespie, B. W., & Chen, S. Y.-P. (2019). *Urban nature experiences reduce stress in the context of daily life based on salivary biomarkers.* Frontiers in Psychology, 10, 722. https://doi.org/10.3389/fpsyg.2019.00722

This study explored biomarkers of stress to better understand administering a "nature pill", i.e. the duration of nature micro-doses, with the greatest benefits experienced between 20-30 minutes

Cox, D. T. C., Shanahan, D. F., Hudson, H. L., Plummer, K. E., Siriwardena, G. M., Fuller, R. A., Anderson, K., Hancock, S., & Gaston, K. J. (2017). *Doses of neighbourhood nature: The benefits for mental health of living with nature.* BioScience, 67(2), 147–155. https://doi.org/10.1093/biosci/biw173

This study aimed to establish the dose requirements of nearby nature for a wide variety of health benefits, and found that depression, social cohesion, physical activity and nature orientation, all improved with increased frequency and duration of exposure to nature.

White, M. P., Alcock, I., Grellier, J., Wheeler, B. W., Hartig, T., Warber, S. L., Bone, A., Depledge, M. H., & Fleming, L. E. (2019). *Spending at least 120 minutes a week in nature is associated with good health and wellbeing.* Scientific Reports, 9, 7730. https://doi.org/10.1038/s41598-019-44097-3

This study found that spending at least 120 minutes in nature each week increased the likelihood of participants reporting good health or high wellbeing.

CREATIVITY

Magsamen, S., & Ross, I. (2023). *Your brain on art: How the arts transform us.* Canongate Books Ltd.

Acar, Selcuk & Tadık, Harun & Myers, Danielle & Sman, Carian & Uysal, Recep. (2020). *Creativity and Wellbeing: A Meta-analysis.* The Journal of Creative Behavior, 55, 738-751. https://doi.org/10.1002/jocb.485

This meta-analysis makes the connection between creative activities and behaviour and wellbeing shifting from an idea of the "mad genius" to a positive psychology framework.

Mansfield, L. et al. (2024) *Creativity and pathways to wellbeing: A rapid scoping review for The What Works Centre for Wellbeing.* https://whatworkswellbeing.org/projects/creativity-and-wellbeing/

A rapid scoping review conducted with the University of the Arts and Brunel University explored the links between creativity and wellbeing and found positive effects that included "reduced anxiety, depression and stress, improved emotions and moods and emotions, high levels of self-esteem, self-efficacy and self-awareness, and improved quality of life."

Keyes, H., Gradidge, S., Forwood, S. E., Gibson, N., Harvey, A., Kis, E., Mutsatsa, K., Ownsworth, R., Roeloffs, S., & Zawisza, M. (2024). *Creating arts and crafting positively predicts subjective wellbeing,* Frontiers in Public Health, 12. https://doi.org/10.3389/fpubh.2024.1417997

A survey exploring how engaging creative arts and crafting predicted subjective wellbeing and loneliness found increased life satisfaction.

Frontier Economics. (2024). *Culture and heritage capital: Monetising the impact of culture and heritage on health and wellbeing.* Department for Culture, Media and Sport (DCMS). https://assets.publishing.service.gov.uk/media/678e2ecf432c55fe2988f615/rpt_-_Frontier_Health_and_Wellbeing_Final_Report_09_12_24_accessible_final.pdf

This report from Frontiers Economics commissioned by The Department for Culture, Media and Sport (DCMS) highlights how adult mental wellbeing is positively impacted by engaging in the arts

CONNECTION

Murthy, V. H. (2023). *Our epidemic of loneliness and isolation: The U.S. Surgeon General's advisory on the healing effects of social connection and community.* U.S. Department of Health and Human Services. https://www.hhs.gov/sites/default/files/surgeon-general-social-connection-advisory.pdf

Holt-Lunstad, J., Smith, T. B., & Layton, J. B. (2010). *Social relationships and mortality risk: A meta-analytic review.* PLoS Medicine, 7(7), e1000316.
https://doi.org/10.1371/journal.pmed.1000316

This meta-analysis highlights that loneliness has as much influence on mortality as other risk factors like smoking.

Baek, E. C., Hyon, R., López, K., Du, M., Porter, M. A., & Parkinson, C. (2023). *Lonely individuals process the world in idiosyncratic ways.* Psychological Science, 34(6), 683–695.
https://doi.org/10.1177/09567976221145316

This study found that lonely people process the world in idiosyncratic ways, particularly in areas of shared perspectives and subjective understanding.

Department for Culture, Media & Sport. (2024, December 4). *Community Life Survey 2023/24: Background and headline findings.* GOV.UK.
https://www.gov.uk/government/statistics/community-life-survey-202324-annual-publication/community-life-survey-202324-background-and-headline-findings

Our adaptation of 'The Circle of Friends' exercise is based on a widely used tool in coaching that originally came out of disability support groups in the 80s and 90s.

Sun, J., Harris, K., & Vazire, S. (2019). *Is well-being associated with the quantity and quality of social interactions?* Journal of Personality and Social Psychology, 119.
https://doi.org/10.1037/pspp0000272

This study attests that both the quality of our relationships – in sense of relatedness and depth of connection – and the quantity, as in frequency, determine the wellbeing benefits of social connection.

Sandstrom, G. M., & Dunn, E. W. (2014). *Social interactions and well-being: The surprising power of weak ties.* Personality and Social Psychology Bulletin, 40(7), 910–922.
https://pubmed.ncbi.nlm.nih.gov/24769739/

This study found that weak ties, such as acquaintances, contribute to people's social and emotional wellbeing.

Waldinger, R. J., & Schulz, M. S. (2023). *The good life: Lessons from the world's longest scientific study of happiness.* Simon & Schuster.
https://www.adultdevelopmentstudy.org

Since 1938, The Harvard Study of Adult Development has tracked the wellbeing of its participants, and determined that the most important contributor to health and happiness levels is the quality of our relationships.

MIND & BODY

Mikkelsen, K., Stojanovska, L., Polenakovic, M., Bosevski, M., & Apostolopoulos, V. (2017). *Exercise and mental health.* Maturitas, 106, 48–56.
https://doi.org/10.1016/j.maturitas.2017.09.003

This article summarises the connection between exercise and mental health, highlighting that exercise improves anxiety, depression and stress, decreases inflammation, and improves psychological and physiological functions.

Chekroud, S. R., Gueorguieva, R., Zheutlin, A. B., Paulus, M., Krumholz, H. M., Krystal, J. H., & Chekroud, A. M. (2018). *Association between physical exercise and mental health in 1·2 million individuals in the USA between 2011 and 2015: A cross-sectional study.* Lancet Psychiatry, 5(9), 739–746.
https://doi.org/10.1016/S2215-0366(18)30227-X

This cross-sectional study found that individuals who exercised had less poor mental health days in the past month than those who didn't and that exercise is associated with "a lower mental health burden."

Fox, K. R. (1999). *The influence of physical activity on mental well-being.* Public Health Nutrition, 2(3a), 411–418. https://doi.org/10.1017/S1368980099000567

    This narrative review highlights how moderate physical activity can improve general mental wellbeing, reduce anxiety and improve self-esteem.

Alnawwar, M. A., Alraddadi, M. I., Algethmi, R. A., Salem, G. A., Salem, M. A., & Alharbi, A. A. (2023). *The effect of physical activity on sleep quality and sleep disorder: A systematic review.* Cureus, 15(8), e43595. https://doi.org/10.7759/cureus.43595

    A systematic review highlighting how regular physical activity can improve sleep quality.

KINDNESS

Hammond, C. (2022). *The keys to kindness: How to be kinder to yourself, others, and the world.* Canongate Books.
    According to the Mental Health Foundation, kindness benefits both the giver and the receiver, increasing happiness and fostering social connection, though we often underestimate its effect.

Yeung, J. W. K., Zhang, Z., & Kim, T. Y. (2018). *Volunteering and health benefits in general adults: Cumulative effects and forms.* BMC Public Health, 18, 8. https://doi.org/10.1186/s12889-017-4561-8

    This study explores how volunteering can be part of a healthy lifestyle by focusing on outcomes like mental and physical health, life satisfaction, social wellbeing and depression.

Kumar, A., & Epley, N. (2023). *A little good goes an unexpectedly long way: Underestimating the positive impact of kindness on recipients.* Journal of Experimental Psychology: General, 152(1), 236–252. https://doi.org/10.1037/xge0001271

    This study highlights how givers underestimate the positive impact of random acts of kindness on recipients.

FUN & PLAY

Brown, S., & Vaughan, C. (2009). *Play: How it shapes the brain, opens the imagination, and invigorates the soul.* Avery.

O'Brien, E., & Seydel, A. (2022). *The power of play: Optimize your joy potential.* Live Life Happy Publishing.

Rucker, M. (2024). *The fun habit: How the pursuit of joy and wonder can change your life.* Atria Books.

Fredrickson, B. L. (1998). *What Good Are Positive Emotions?* Review of General Psychology, 2(3), 300-319. https://doi.org/10.1037/1089-2680.2.3.300

    This article introduces the broaden-and-build theory of positive emotions, that people experience positive emotions like joy, contentment and interest to broaden their "momentary thought-action repertoire" that in turn builds their intellectual, physical and social resources.

Ho, W. W. Y. (2022). *Influence of play on positive psychological development in emerging adulthood: A serial mediation model.* Frontiers in Psychology, 13, Article 1057557. https://doi.org/10.3389/fpsyg.2022.1057557

    A serial mediation model that shows that experiences of play in emerging adulthood cultivates emotional intelligence and improves resilience.

Farley, A., Kennedy-Behr, A., & Brown, T. (2020). *An investigation into the relationship between playfulness and well-being in Australian adults: An exploratory study.* OTJR: Occupation, Participation and Health, 41(1), 56–64. https://doi.org/10.1177/1539449220945311

    This study found that playfulness nurtures an individual's wellbeing, through highlighting the positive relationship between play and positive emotions, engagement with others, identifying meaning in one's life and overall wellbeing.

Keltner, D. (2023). *Awe: The transformative power of everyday wonder.* Penguin Random House.

May, K. (2023). *Enchantment: A memoir.* Riverhead Books

Monroy, M., & Keltner, D. (2023). *Awe as a pathway to mental and physical health.* Perspectives on Psychological Science, 18(2), 309–320.
https://doi.org/10.1177/17456916221094856

In this article, the authors propose that awe promotes mental and physical health through five processes that arise in nature, spirituality, collective movement, music and psychedelics.

Monroy, M., Amster, M., Eagle, J., Zerwas, F. K., Keltner, D., & López, J. E. (2025). *Awe reduces depressive symptoms and improves well-being in a randomized-controlled clinical trial.* Scientific reports, 15(1), 16453.
https://doi.org/10.1038/s41598-025-96555-w

This study explores how an awe-intervention can impact psychological health, particularly reducing symptoms of depression and alleviating chronic stress.

Li, J. J., Dou, K., Wang, Y. J., & Nie, Y. G. (2019). *Why awe promotes prosocial behaviors? The mediating effects of future time perspective and self-transcendence meaning of life.* Frontiers in Psychology, 10, 1140.
https://doi.org/10.3389/fpsyg.2019.01140

This study explored the effects of awe on pro-sociality and found that it can enhance people's sense of collective concern and being part of broader social contexts.

Stellar, J. E., John-Henderson, N., Anderson, C. L., Gordon, A. M., McNeil, G. D., & Keltner, D. (2015). *Positive affect and markers of inflammation: discrete positive emotions predict lower levels of inflammatory cytokines.* Emotion (Washington, D.C.), 15(2), 129–133.
https://doi.org/10.1037/emo0000033

This study focused on the impact of positive emotions, such as awe, on people's physical health through examining proinflammatory cytokines, concluding that it was associated with lower levels.

Bai, Y., Ocampo, J., Jin, G., Chen, S., Benet-Martinez, V., Monroy, M., Anderson, C., & Keltner, D. (2021). *Awe, daily stress, and elevated life satisfaction.* Journal of Personality and Social Psychology, 120(4), 837–860.
https://doi.org/10.1037/pspa0000267

This series of studies highlight how experiences of awe can reduce daily stressors and subsequently improve overall sense of life satisfaction.

Sturm, V. E., Datta, S., Roy, A. R. K., Sible, I. J., Kosik, E. L., Veziris, C. R., Chow, T. E., Morris, N. A., Neuhaus, J., Kramer, J. H., Miller, B. L., Holley, S. R., & Keltner, D. (2022). *Big smile, small self: Awe walks promote prosocial positive emotions in older adults.* Emotion (Washington, D.C.), 22(5), 1044–1058.
https://doi.org/10.1037/emo0000876

This study investigated how "awe-walks" taken by older adults can increase positive social emotions and mitigate the decline in social disconnection, anxiety and sadness common in this age group.

Rudd, M., Vohs, K. D., & Aaker, J. (2012). *Awe expands people's perception of time, alters decision making, and enhances well-being.* Psychological Science, 23(10), 1130–1136.
https://doi.org/10.1177/0956797612438731

This study discovered several benefits in people who have a greater sense of awe related to time-perception from feeling like they had more time to being more inclined to volunteer to help others.

Gordon, Amie & Anderson, Craig & Piff, Paul & McNeil, Galen & Keltner, Dacher. (2017). *Awe and Humility.* Journal of Personality and Social Psychology. 114.
https://doi.org/10.1037/pspi0000109

This study investigates the connection between awe and humility.

PURPOSE

Mogi, K. (2018). *The little book of ikigai: The secret Japanese way to live a happy and long life.* Quercus.

García, H., & Miralles, F. (2017). *Ikigai: The Japanese secret to a long and happy life.* Penguin Books.

Boreham, I. D., & Schutte, N. S. (2023). *The relationship between purpose in life and depression and anxiety: A meta-analysis.* Journal of clinical psychology, 79(12), 2736–2767.
https://doi.org/10.1002/jclp.23576

A meta-analysis that found that a higher sense of purpose was associated with lower levels of anxiety and depression.

Kim, E. S., Shiba, K., Boehm, J. K., & Kubzansky, L. D. (2020). *Sense of purpose in life and five health behaviors in older adults.* Preventive Medicine, 139, 106172.
https://doi.org/10.1016/j.ypmed.2020.106172

Exploring how purpose affected health behaviours in older adults, this study discovered that those with a higher sense of purpose were less likely to be physically inactive, develop sleep problems and an unhealthy body-mass index.

Sutin, A. R., Luchetti, M., Stephan, Y., Sesker, A. A., & Terracciano, A. (2024). *Purpose in life and stress: An individual-participant meta-analysis of 16 samples.* Journal of Affective Disorders, 345, 378–385.
https://doi.org/10.1016/j.jad.2023.10.149

A meta-analysis that found that having a purpose in life was associated with less subjective feelings of stress.

Bennett, D. A., Schneider, J. A., Buchman, A. S., Barnes, L. L., Boyle, P. A., & Wilson, R. S. (2012). *Overview and findings from the Rush Memory and Aging Project.* Current Alzheimer Research, 9(6), 646–663.
https://doi.org/10.2174/156720512801322663

A longitudinal study into memory and aging that highlights how purpose in life is associated with a reduced risk of Alzheimer's Disease and mild cognitive impairment as well as a slower rate of cognitive decline in people without dementia.

Sinek, S. (2010, May). *How great leaders inspire action* [Video]. TED Conferences.
https://www.ted.com/talks/simon_sinek_how_great_leaders_inspire_action

Ness Labs. (n.d.). *Purpose anxiety.* https://nesslabs.com/purpose-anxiety

Permission to use the Ikigai model provided by Marc Winn at Penguin House USA https://theviewinside.me/the-story-behind-the-ikigai-venn-diagram-a-personal-journey/"

SPIRITUALITY

Ter Kuile, C. (2020). *The power of ritual: Turning everyday activities into soulful practices.* HarperOne.

Yaden, D. B., Batz-Barbarich, C. L., Ng, V., et al. (2022). *A meta-analysis of religion/spirituality and life satisfaction.* Journal of Happiness Studies, 23, 4147–4163.
https://doi.org/10.1007/s10902-022-00558-7

This meta-analysis of religion/spirituality and life satisfaction found that amongst five dimensions including spirituality, religious practices and religious/spiritual experiences there was a significant and positive correlation.

Subbotsky, E. (2014). *The belief in magic in the age of science.* SAGE Open, 4(1).
https://doi.org/10.1177/2158244014521433

This article suggests that a belief in magic is a "property of the human mind", and makes the difference between the benefits of magical thinking and magical beliefs as psychological constructs.

Hobson, N. M., Bonk, D., & Inzlicht, M. (2017). *Rituals decrease the neural response to performance failure.* PeerJ, 5, e3363.
https://doi.org/10.7717/peerj.3363

This examination found that rituals act as a buffer against uncertainty and anxiety and regulate how people's brains respond to personal failure.

Lang, M., Krátký, J., & Xygalatas, D. (2020). *The role of ritual behaviour in anxiety reduction: An investigation of Marathi religious practices in Mauritius.* Philosophical Transactions of the Royal Society B, 375(1805), 20190431.
https://doi.org/10.1098/rstb.2019.0431

This study investigates how engaging in ritual can lower perceived and physiological anxiety.

Norton, M. I., & Gino, F. (2014). *Rituals alleviate grieving for loved ones, lovers, and lotteries.* Journal of Experimental Psychology: General, 143(1), 266–272.
https://doi.org/10.1037/a0031772

Can mourning rituals alleviate grief? This study identified that rituals help people regain a feeling of control which helps reduce their sense of loss.

Pew Research Center. (2023). *Spirituality among Americans.*
https://www.pewresearch.org/religion/2023/12/07/spirituality-among-americans/

UNTETHERING

Veissière, S. P. L., & Stendel, M. (2018). *Hypernatural monitoring: A social rehearsal account of smartphone addiction.* Frontiers in Psychology, 9.
https://doi.org/10.3389/fpsyg.2018.00141

This study attempts to counter the idea of smartphone addiction as antisocial and rather frames it within a fundamental human need around connectedness: to monitor and be monitored by others.

Putri, D., Andini, S., Ingtyas, F., & Sabrina, E. (2024). *Meta-analysis: The impact of technological advancements on social interaction in the digital era.* Journal Corner of Education, Linguistics, and Literature, 4, 29–39.
https://doi.org/10.54012/jcell.v4i001.359

Exploring how technology effects social interactions, this meta-analysis highlights both positive (such as expanding social networks) and negative impacts (reduced face-to-face interactions).

Augner, C., Vlasak, T., Aichhorn, W., & Barth, A. (2021). *The association between problematic smartphone use and symptoms of anxiety and depression: A meta-analysis.* Journal of Public Health, 45.
https://doi.org/10.1093/pubmed/fdab350

A meta-analysis exploring problematic smartphone use and anxiety and/or depression that found that the former could be seen as an indicator of symptoms for the latter.

Yousef, A. M. F., Alshamy, A., Tlili, A., & Metwally, A. H. S. (2025). *Demystifying the new dilemma of brain rot in the digital era: A review.* Brain Sciences, 15(3), 283.
https://doi.org/10.3390/brainsci15030283

A meta-analysis that aimed to explore the digital phenomenon of "brain rot" that highlights how it can lead to emotional desensitisation, impaired executive functioning skills, and negative behaviours.

IF LOST START HERE®

First published by **FROM YOU TO ME LTD** in January 2026

For a full range of all our titles where gifts can also be personalised, please visit

WWW.FROMYOUTOME.COM

FROM YOU TO ME are committed to a sustainable future for our business, our customers and our planet. This book is printed and bound on FSC® certified paper in Shenzhen, China in January 2026.